The HOT CHICKEN Cookbook

The HOT CHICKEN Cookbook

THE FIERY HISTORY & RED-HOT RECIPES OF NASHVILLE'S BELOVED BIRD

BY TIMOTHY CHARLES DAVIS

SPRING HOUSE PRESS

CONTENTS

CHAPTER 3
**78 WONDER BREAD TO WHITE LINEN:
HOT CHICKEN LEAVES THE ROOST**

Recipes

Personalities

Miscellany

CHAPTER 4
**119 THE COOL DOWN:
DESSERTS THAT OFFER SWEET RELIEF**

Recipes

FOREWORD

by Carla Hall

Hot Chicken has long deserved a devotee such as Timothy Davis to put together a definitive guide to the history, recipes, and culture surrounding this Southern specialty. Every day this fiery dish is finding new fans across the country in restaurants, food trucks, picnic baskets, cookbooks, television shows, and good, old-fashioned shared family meals. Consider this cookbook your road atlas for the discovery of a food culture rich in history. From chefs to politicians to musicians, Tim has tracked down insights from those most passionate about Hot Chicken and shares the origins of their

Hot Chicken passions, along with great tips like the Ten Commandments of Hot Chicken.

The cacophony of information that has been compiled here through stories and recipes, and with vibrant photos, is a wonderful representation of the richness of Hot Chicken culture. Timothy truly puts our finger on the pulse of Nashville's delicacy, the history, the levels of heat, the diehard community that surrounds it, the culture that it has created, and the dishes that have been inspired in the wake of its lure.

Some like it hot. Some like it hotter.

INTRODUCTION
by Andrew Zimmern

I'm blessed. I've been eating Hot Chicken—or what the rest of the world calls Nashville Hot Chicken—for 40 years, ever since my dad first took me to the Music City on one of his business trips, and we swung by Prince's Hot Chicken Shack for a half dozen pieces of "hot" served with white bread and pickles. Technically, extra pickles, since that's the only way my dad ate Hot Chicken . . . with lots and lots of pickles.

I love fried chicken, but I really love the

Hot Chicken that they serve in Nashville. The bodily intake of extra oil—a given considering the cooking technique—the heat of the chiles (typically cayenne), and the mandatory infantile joking about the "hotter on the way out than on the way in" factor are my kind of bonus issues. The last time I ate at Prince's, I had lunch there with Lorrie Morgan and Andre Prince. They asked me where I was headed and as I got up from our table, I told them I was on my way to the airport. Andre slapped her leg, giggling, and said she felt sorry for the people sitting around me.

In all seriousness, there is something holy and communal about sharing a nicely fried platter of yardbird, especially one with such a great story. Food is great, but food with a story is even better. With the gospel of Nashville Hot

Chicken going global, books like this one and hundreds of restaurants in and around Tennessee serving the stuff (Hattie B's is my new favorite), it's a great time to hear these stories, because it makes the eating so much more delightful. My most recent one goes like this.

Last time I was in Nashville, I got the opportunity to stand in the kitchens of Hattie B's and Prince's on the same day and watch the stuff cook. Later that night I got to watch Erik Anderson, then the chef at Nashville's Catbird Seat, cook and serve me his inspirational version of it. I loved them all. And the overall effect was a perspective-changer. Hot Chicken's general ingredients are all essentially the same, but the outcomes of the marriage of ingredient and technique result in widely divergent plates of food. Pre-seasoning or brining, dredging or battering, frying and then seasoning again with a cayenne pepper sauce or paste rubbed or pressed into the crispy coating: They all look like Hot Chicken, but they aren't the same.

At Hattie B's, three generations of the Bishop family take pride in the insane quality of their bespoke bird. And it shows—despite being the new kids in town, they have the experience to make a superior bird. The tile and the stainless steel in the kitchen was spotless. The bird was perfection. Moist and tender, tasting of real poultry and sheathed in a crispy brown mantle of skin and batter, pressed and rubbed with their version of the classic pepper "paste" that all good Hot Chicken comes bathed in. For me, it's still the plate I measure all others against. And don't skip that pimento mac n' cheese!

At Prince's, they used to use skillets for their chicken frying, but now they use a fleet of deep fryers, using some of the oil they fry in to loosen the chile paste for a robust slather after the bird comes out of the fryer and into the seasoning bowl. This is the old world experience, befitting a roadside joint that's been in business for over 75 years. And a small concession to keep the supply of Hot Chicken rolling out the door feeding lines that are long at lunch and dinner, and even longer late in the evening!

Those lines started in the 1930s when Thornton Prince, the great uncle of current owner Andre Prince Jeffries, first opened his chicken shack. According to Jeffries, the creation of Hot Chicken was a lucky accident. Apparently great-uncle Thornton was quite the ladies' man, and after a night spent with his then-girlfriend, she cooked him a fried chicken breakfast with buckets of extra hot pepper as revenge for his womanizing. Ironically, Thornton decided he loved the stuff and with his brothers opened the BBQ Chicken Shack Café. That was almost 85 years ago.

Food is great. Food with a story is better. Food with a story you haven't heard before is best of all. Nashville Hot Chicken has been captivating our attention as a culture for generations because it's been incubated in secret, under hyper-local circumstances. So now, as the story unfolds, the thrill is going global, and influencing a whole world of chefs and eaters.

Standing in the kitchen at Catbird Seat with Erik, with plates of Prince's and Hattie B's hot chicken still sweating out of my pores, I watched a world-class modernist chef, a carpetbagging Midwestern restaurateur, serve me a two-bite portion of Hot Chicken skin with Wonder Bread emulsion and a homemade pickle that might be the best taste of Hot Chicken I've ever had. It got me thinking: How many other foods are that inspirational, that revelatory of a place and an attitude of a city, a food with a story so powerful that young rock star chefs can't wait to put their version up on the line? That's what Hot Chicken is all about. Andre put it best once in an interview with the Southern Foodways Alliance when she said it's "old school," which, to me, is always best.

"This chicken cannot be rushed; it cannot be rushed. To be right it takes time. And then sometimes when we give it to the customers too fast they don't want it; they think something is wrong with it 'cause they're used to waiting. So I find that rather odd, but—that's the way they expect it 'cause that's the way it usually is but it takes time to cook the chicken right. It's not a fast-food; we're definitely not a fast-food restaurant. It's old-time; it's like old-school."

FOOD IS GREAT. FOOD WITH A STORY IS BETTER. FOOD WITH A STORY YOU HAVEN'T HEARD BEFORE IS BEST OF ALL.

CHAPTER ONE

THE ORIGIN(S) OF HOT CHICKEN

REVENGE IS A DISH BEST SERVED. . . HOT

The generally-agreed-upon story goes like this: Thornton Prince III—a "roamer" according to his grand-niece—came home late one evening, which, in and of itself, was nothing new. Prince was a handsome man, lanky and long-armed, but well-put-together thanks to the years of manual labor he'd endured as a sharecropper's son. ➡

Prince's rampant carousing had aroused the ire of his girlfriend(s) before, but this time it sparked a fire he couldn't contain. His girlfriend at the time had heard it all before: the excuses, the fact-fudging, the flat-out falsehoods. Finally she decided enough was enough, and began to hatch a plan that would focus his wandering eyes.

Exhausted by it all, and bent on revenge, she set about her kitchen, eyeing the options. Knives were a no-go. But there are other ways to hurt a man, we can imagine her thinking, and if the way to a man's heart is indeed through his stomach, then maybe it was high time to make his burn.

There's an old axiom that revenge is a dish best served cold. Prince's girlfriend took the opposite tact. Sometime the next morning, she made him his favorite, a fried chicken breakfast. Only she knows exactly the process she went through to spice the bird to the point where it caused pain worthy of a punishment, but suffice it to say that it involved a heaping helping of cayenne pepper. The goal was to light him up, make him feel as red-hot as her heretofore-repressed rage.

Then a weird thing happened: He liked it. He loved it, in fact. He loved it so much that he immediately set about attempts to replicate it. Again, the exact preparation is guarded and may have evolved in the passing years, but once he zeroed in on a preparation he liked—and flush with laudatory nods from friends and family—Thornton decided

Start at the source. The staple at legendary Prince's is fried chicken served mysteriously hot and always on white bread, with pickles.

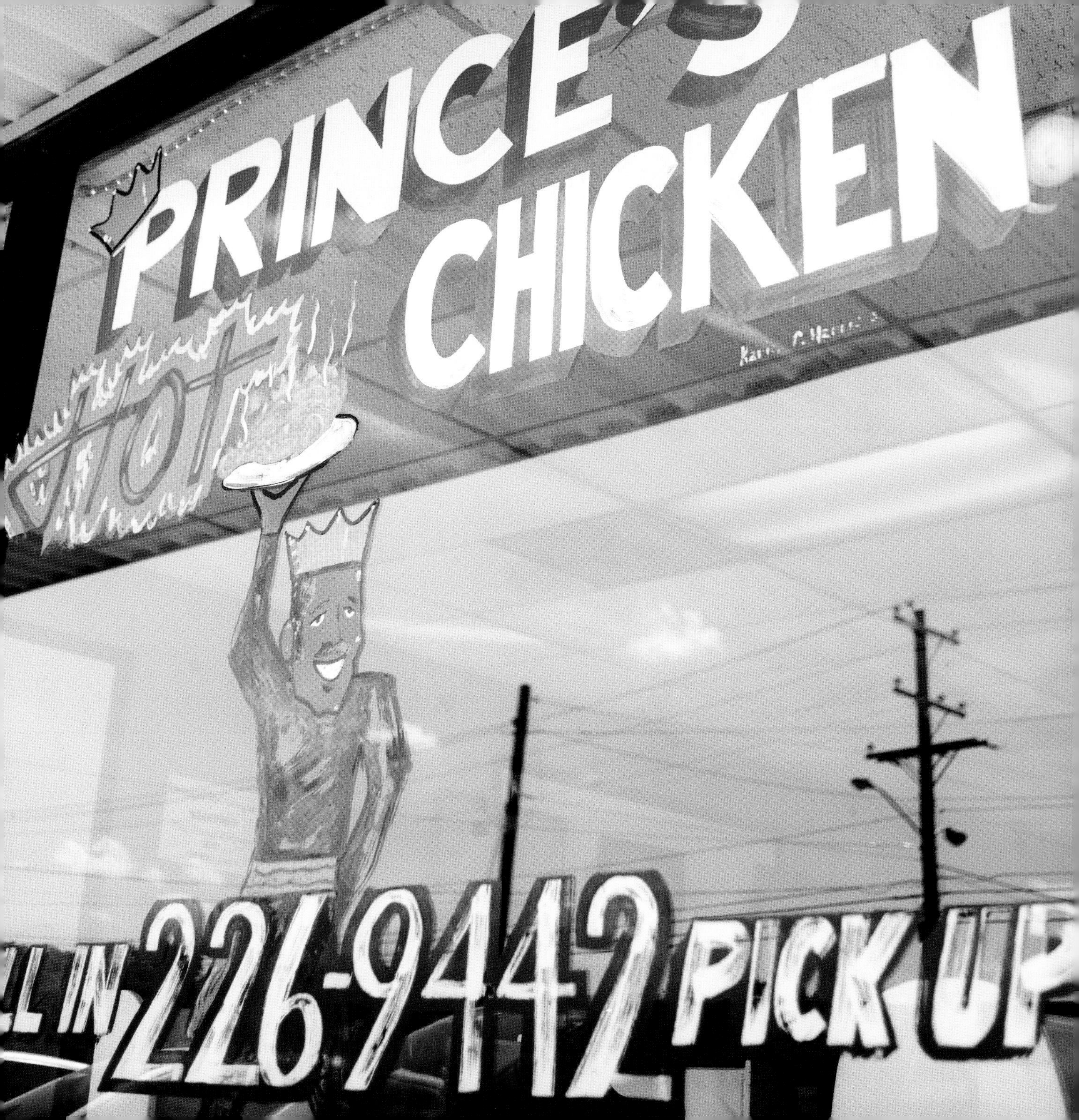
PRINCE'S
CHICKEN
HOT
226-9442 PICK UP

★MAINS★
TRADITIONAL HOT CHICKEN
The familiar spice with a few secret ingredients of its own

Most every Hot Chicken devotee has his or her own recipe, and the ingredients are always closely guarded. This Hot Chicken recipe is traditional in flavor and spice but includes dry mustard and sugar. While mustard and sugar don't pop up in many published recipes, I wouldn't be surprised to find them hidden on the spice rack at many Hot Chicken shacks. The mustard lends pungency and the sugar helps round out the flavor. The rub and paste used here can be used to accomodate most any degree of heat. For more heat, simply use more of each.

PREPARATION

Fill an iron skillet or Dutch oven about 2 inches deep with oil and heat to 350°. Mix the flour and a tablespoon of the spice mix (use the paste recipe, except for the oil) in a paper grocery sack. Working in small batches, drop the chicken into the bag, shake, let rest briefly, and shake again. Test the oil by sprinkling a small pinch of flour into it—when ready the oil should gently bubble around the flour. Carefully lower the chicken into the oil. Fry only a few pieces at a time so as not to crowd the pan. Cover partially and cook until one side begins to brown. Turn the chicken and cook until golden brown. (Internal temperature should be at least 165°.) Remove from the oil and drain on a wire rack or paper towels. Cook in batches until all is done.

Ingredients for the paste are for what most would consider medium heat. To add heat, simply add more cayenne to the mix. To make the paste, heat your bacon fat (or use a couple teaspoons of the just-used fry oil) and add a little at a time to the spices listed for the paste. What you're looking to achieve is a brushable consistency that is neither a hard paste nor too liquid-y; aim for something along the lines of stone-ground mustard. Liberally brush the finished chicken with the paste. Grab a thick stack of napkins. Enjoy.

INGREDIENTS
8 TO 10 SERVINGS

- 1 whole fryer, cut up
- 2 cups all purpose flour
- 2 tablespoons rub (recipe below)
- Peanut oil (or frying oil of your choice)

FOR THE PASTE

- 3 tablespoons cayenne pepper
- 1½ teaspoons sea salt
- 2 teaspoons dry mustard
- 1 teaspoon sugar
- 1 teaspoon smoked or hot paprika
- 1 teaspoon freshly ground black pepper
- ¾ teaspoon garlic powder
- Bacon fat or used oil, as needed for paste

to bring Hot Chicken into the world, via a tiny little eatery called, at that time, BBQ Chicken Shack.

Did Thornton Prince invent Hot Chicken as we know it today? Almost assuredly not. Some pepperhead had surely napalmed his or her yardbird before, whether inadvertently or through divine inspiration. What's more, other cultures have been making incendiary chicken dishes for eons. Also, it's instructive to remember that, if you take the Prince's Hot Chicken origin story at face value, it was Thornton Prince's girlfriend who deserves the lion's share of credit for the

The Early Days. A recently discovered picture (below) shows Thornton Prince III (far right), the man responsible for Hot Chicken's creation. At left, the original register from the first location.

★ON THE SIDE★
SPICY TURNIP GREENS

Is it even possible to eat Hot Chicken without greens?

Eddie Hernandez of Decatur, Georgia's Taqueria del Sol (and its sister franchises in Decatur, Athens, and Nashville) makes a tasty cross-cultural version of turnip greens at his low-key, high-flavor eateries. Adapted from his recipe, this take on classic turnip greens fairly sizzles with flavor, taking an old standby and giving it the hot rod treatment: if you ever thought turnip greens were about as exciting as your grandmother's tired old Plymouth, allow Chef Eddie to add a little rocket fuel to the proceedings.

PREPARATION

Begin by cooking greens with water and pork fat for 45 minutes. Then melt the butter in a large, heavy pot over medium-high heat. Stir in the onions and cook until softened, stirring often, about 8 minutes. Stir in the garlic and chile de arbol and cook, stirring constantly, for 1 minute. Stir in the tomatoes, greens, and chicken stock. Increase the heat to high and bring to a boil. Reduce the heat to medium/low and simmer, partially covered, until the flavors are blended and the greens are heated through—about 15 minutes. Season with salt to taste. Serve hot.

INGREDIENTS
8 TO 10 SERVINGS

- 6 cups cleaned, chopped and cooked turnip greens (about 6 bundles)
- 1 cup chopped onion
- ½ cup chopped garlic
- 1 tablespoon ground chile de arbol or ground cayenne pepper
- 1½ cups diced tomatoes
- 4 tablespoons butter
- 3 cups chicken stock
- 2 teaspoons salt

A GAME OF (HOT) CHICKEN

A few words from Edward Lee of Louisville's 610 Magnolia

Ed Lee's excellent *Smoke & Pickles: Recipes and Stories from a New Southern Kitchen* and his signature Louisville restarurants—610 Magnolia and MilkWood—are celebrations of unexpected but perfect combinations of flavor. If you've seen Lee on any of his television appearances (*Top Chef, Iron Chef America, Foodography,* and more) you won't be surprised to read his enthusiastic take on Prince's and Nashville's iconic dish.

Going to Prince's in Nashville is not about going to eat fried chicken, it's about making a fucking pilgrimage, a rite of passage, a badge of honor. I was so anxious and giddy my first time, I ignored the advice of the seasoned regulars in line around me and ordered the extra hot. I had to sit there and take down the whole meal while the staff laughed at me. Throughout the pain, the flavor kept bringing me back for another bite until there was nothing but bones left on my plate and a burning sensation creeping down my chest.

I've been back countless times since then, and each time, I gain a new appreciation. There have been many imitations, and most are really good in their own way, but there's only one Prince's. It's not just about the chicken, you see. It's the inconvenient traffic to get there, the fleeting friendships you make while waiting in line, it's going to the shop next door and getting a stack of bootleg hip-hop CDs, it's about the white bread stained bloodred from the chili oil, it's the painful regret sitting in bed late that night knowing your own stomach is revolting against your decisions. It's knowing that there is nothing more egalitarian and communal than standing on line with people that share a passion for the deliciousness and pain that defines an experience at Prince's. I can't wait to go back.

—Edward Lee

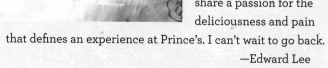

now-fetishized food's creation.

What Thornton Prince almost assuredly did do was refine Hot Chicken's preparation, popularize it, and make a bit of peppery payback into something bigger—bigger than himself, of course, and ultimately bigger than his beloved Nashville. He had no way of knowing all this at the time. He just knew he loved that hellfire-hot fried chicken. And if he loved it, others might too.

SOME THINGS NEVER CHANGE

These days Simone Jeffries runs Prince's Hot Chicken with her mother, Andre. Simone laughs when told this particular take on the restaurant's origin story, having heard myriad variations on the tale.

"Allegedly, that's how all this came into play," she says. "I'd rather just leave it at that. The Prince men are quite handsome, and most of them liked the ladies!"

The truth is, no one is really certain how Nashville-style Hot Chicken came to be, including the Prince family. People seldom saved things like menus, newspaper clippings, and other memorabilia as they often do today. Truth is, many people didn't have all that much back then worth saving. People were trying *escape* their past, not document it. "Upwardly mobile" more often than not translated to "keeping one's head above water."

Why keep reminders of that past around? The Princes were focused on feeding people, not feeding a story. At that time, the story wouldn't mean a whit to the popular food media, because there *was* no popular food media. The restaurants that did get press decades ago were high-end, white tablecloth places, not workingman's joints peopled by African Americans.

Not a lot of flash. 70-year-old wooden booths, handwritten signs, and the occasional framed article make up Prince's dining room.

★ON THE SIDE★
SKILLET-FRIED OKRA
A shame this Southern staple is seldom seen elsewhere

INGREDIENTS
4 SERVINGS

- 1 lb. small okra pods
- 4 tablespoons bacon drippings (or peanut or vegetable oil)
- ½ cup cornmeal
- Freshly ground black pepper
- 1 teaspoon Kosher salt

To those not from the American South (or from Africa, from whence it originally came), okra can be a bit of a hard sell: Boiled or sauteed, it can be forbiddingly slimy and, by itself, it's somewhat tasteless. Dust in it cornmeal and fry it in a cast-iron skillet, however, and a magical transformation happens.

PREPARATION

Trim and slice the okra into ¼ inch to ¾ inch thick rounds. Rinse under running water in a colander and let drain. Mix together corn meal and salt and pepper. Heat a cast iron skillet to medium high and add the fat. Combine okra with the cornmeal mixture and toss to coat evenly. Distribute battered okra evenly around the bottom of the skillet. Lower heat to medium and cook for seven to eight minutes, or until golden brown, stirring often. Transfer to paper towel-lined plate to cool.

"We can't really pinpoint the date, as far as to exactly when my family opened up the Chicken Shack," says Andre Prince Jeffries, third-generation owner and operator of Prince's and the de facto public face of Hot Chicken.

"It was on 28th and Jefferson St., at that period of time, and then it moved downtown to 9th and Cedar. And then to 17th and Jo Johnston Avenue, (then to) 28th and Clarksville Highway, then to here."

"Here" is 123 Ewing Drive, just off of Dickerson Pike, tucked between a tanning salon and a place that, if it were in New York City, would be called a bodega. So Prince's is in a strip mall, and not a particularly pretty one at that. It is home, however, and has been for some time.

"I know my mom got the restaurant when I was 12," Simone says. "So she's had it since 1980. She actually got it from Maude Prince [the wife of William Prince, Thornton's brother]. My mom always said she wanted a restaurant. She said she had a dream that she started a restaurant, and it was packed to the gills. We used to go to California every summer, because my uncle lived out there. She said on one of our trips back from California she had that dream."

Andre Prince Jeffries' dream became a reality sooner than even she expected.

"I was the only one in my immediate family who was divorced at that time," says Andre, "and my mother and father [Wilhelmina and Bruce Prince] just started taking care of me. I was working with Metro Nashville at the courthouse. So I got into this business. We didn't come to the Chicken Shack as children, because this was a late-night place. It always opened up at 6 o'clock in the evening. We always had outside jobs, main jobs. This was something they did to just try and keep it in the family."

Business acumen—or lack of it—was counterbalanced, she says, by a lifelong love of her new restaurant's calling card.

"On Sunday mornings, black families back then would have a big meal," she says, smiling. "A big ol' meal. I guess that's the time they didn't have to work the fields, or whatever they did to pay a bill. So Sundays were our only time to get together and have a meal. And it'd usually be in a buffet style. It was a big ol' Sunday feast. Those who went to

 Worth the wait. You can call it in or order at the window and have a seat. Either way, the line gets long and nothing rushes the food.

I CAN HEAR THE HEAT BEATING AS ONE

Yo La Tengo's Ira Kaplan on Hot Chicken

In indie music circles, Ira Kaplan is viewed as something of an elder statesman of the scene—the kind of elder statesman who will still melt your face with a searing, staccato guitar attack roughly eight-to-10 times a show. As co-founder, vocalist, guitarist, and lead songwriter of the American indie rock band Yo La Tengo—not to mention a talented journalist—Kaplan often has his hands full. However, he readily took a few minutes to discuss Hot Chicken. He's a keen fan of the the dish, having first tasted it when recording in Nashville. How big of a fan? He's named multiple songs after the stuff.

I read that another band turned you onto Hot Chicken. Do you remember who the band was? Can you describe your first impressions?

Richard Baluyut from the New York band Versus told us about Prince's. He had been there while on tour. James (Mc-New, bassist for Yo La Tengo) and I went there. We didn't know anything. We were told it came in mild, medium, hot, and extra-hot, but if we'd never been there before, we would not be allowed to have extra-hot. We asked if we could at least taste "extra-hot sauce." What rubes we were—we were informed that there is no sauce. I can't remember what James ordered, but I know I ordered a half chicken, hot. I found it simultaneously delicious and practically inedible—I ate a piece a day for four days.

You've immortalized the dish in song. Was there a talismanic quality behind the name that inspired you? Just a random, we-need-a-title kind of situation, perhaps?

It was definitely not a we-need-a-title situation, as we used it as a subtitle at first. The words "Hot Chicken" struck us as musical, and we liked weaving our experience of recording

in Nashville into the record (we found the title of our album *Electr-o-pura* on a visit to the Museum of Beverage Containers on a day off from recording). It was also an allusion to "Hot Burrito #1" and "2" on (The Flying Burrito Brothers') *The Gilded Palace of Sin*. When we named a subsequent song "Return to Hot Chicken"—an instrumental that, by the time we named it, had been placed as the lead track on our record *I Can Hear the Heart Beating as One*—we were essentially calling it "Return to Nashville."

How do you feel about the spread of Hot Chicken to NYC, Philadelphia, Chicago, and the like? Have you tried it at any of these places? What were your impressions?

I don't believe I've ever eaten Hot Chicken anywhere other than Prince's. If I did, it certainly didn't make an impression.

church were glad to dress up and put on a nice outfit instead of getting up and putting on the same old ripped work clothes. But my father would have this chicken, in this greasy bag, and it would always be on top of the stove on Sunday morning. He would drive by the Chicken Shack on that Saturday night when we were already in bed because he was a roamer, a little roamer, like my great uncle Thornton. But he always stopped by the Chicken Shack on his

way home, and bring that greasy bag. We'd look for it! Because he didn't bring that much. And getting to have a little of that with our breakfast? Whoo! That was the bomb!"

Jeffries figured that what had worked before would work again. Still, she decided to make a few key changes for the sake of efficiency. She moved the bulk of the chicken frying from cast-iron skillets over to deep fryers, and changed the Shack's name to better reflect not only her family's name, but the restaurants signature specialty: Prince's Hot Chicken Shack.

One thing she kept? Her great-uncle's now-famous wood benches. "They're over 70 years old," she says. "They've been painted over so many times I'm not sure there's any wood left under there. I try and keep all I can. It's sad when you don't have anything to show for your ancestors' hard work."

Andre was equipped, of course, with perhaps the most important part of the whole equation: her family's famous Hot Chicken recipe.

"The base of the recipe is the same," says Andre's daughter Simone. "Some parts of it have been tweaked a little bit because of what you have available in this day and time. But, for the most part, you are still getting the original recipe."

"When I took over in 1980, one of my customers came in and asked why I didn't have something her child could eat," says Andre. "So that's when I started doing the plain, the mild, the medium, the hot, the extra-hot. In my great-uncle's day, it was one way—hot."

Simone Prince says that, despite the restaurant's name, the chicken has never been about the heat element alone, and notes that Thornton's "hot" might be equal to a

 Keep it simple. You can't go wrong with a quarter white or quarter dark, with a pile of sides to tamp down the heat.

★ON THE SIDE★
PIMENTO MAC & CHEESE
Two Southern favorites are even better together

INGREDIENTS
4 SERVINGS

- 3 tablespoons butter
- 3 tablespoons AP flour
- Kosher salt
- 1 quart whole milk
- 1 bay leaf
- ½ teaspoon crushed red pepper
- 8 ounces diced pimentos
- ½ cup extra sharp cheddar cheese (shredded)
- 1 cup macaroni pasta

In its worst, boxed form, mac & cheese is a simple supper for kids or college students, its popularity ranking right up there with ramen noodles. The good stuff—gooey and creamy and cheesy and crusty—is something else altogether. The Bishop family at Hattie B's in Nashville makes theirs with another totemic Southern foodstuff, pimento cheese. The results are sinful without being sordid.

PREPARATION

Melt butter in a medium sauce pot on medium high heat. Once butter is completely melted, whisk in all the flour at once. Turn burner to low. Simmer the roux for 4-5 minutes, stirring occasionally. In a separate pot, heat up the milk with the crushed red pepper, a big pinch of salt, and the bay leaf. Once the milk comes to a simmer, ladle it into the roux, whisking to incorporate. Do this until all the milk is blended in. Add pimentos, juice and all. Simmer the Béchamel sauce for about 10-15 minutes on very low heat, stirring. At the end, add the cheese and stir it in. Do not cook long after you add the cheese; you just want to melt it. Once it is melted, remove from the heat. It is easy to scorch the sauce at this point, which can ruin the whole batch.

Cook pasta in rapidly boiling salted water for 7 minutes (*al dente*). Strain, and place in a bowl. Toss pasta with 1 tablespoon butter. Mix 1 cup of cooked pasta per 1¼ cup of cheese sauce.

Put macaroni and cheese in a baking dish. Bake at 350° for 20-25 minutes. It should be bubbling. Remove from the oven and sprinkle 1 cup of shredded extra sharp cheddar over the top. Bake for about 5 minutes longer, or just long enough to brown the cheese.

Prince's medium today.

"You can always make anything *hot*. You have to find that flavor." Andre says. "You can sprinkle hot sauce or jalapeños on anything. But the hard part's not the hot part, you know? We just fry our chicken. We have wings a few days a week, and Chicken Tender Thursdays. People have asked us to do fish, pork chops, even deep-fry turkeys. But we don't get into that. We'll leave that to others. Stick with what you know, I say."

This extends to sticking with the folks who have stuck with them along the way.

"The older generations who were around when my great-uncles were, they have the greatest stories," Andre says. "This was before desegregation, when blacks had to come through the back. And they reversed it. At the restaurant on Charlotte, the dining room was black, and if you were white, you'd come down the alleyway and sit in an area off the kitchen, in the back. One of these old-timers, who was a white man, said him and his friend had been drinking one day, and came in the front by mistake. He said 'for once I got to feel what they felt, and it kind of changed my perception on things from that point on.' I told him, 'you didn't make a mistake. That was the whole point—to change people's perception.'"

"Repeat customers feel like family to us," Simone says. "People have been coming so long that we've had people, when we get shorthanded, who'll jump in and start working!" The help extends beyond work to family. "I'll always tell my children to behave because it'll get back to me. My oldest daughter is 25, and I tell her that I'll get it through the Prince's grapevine whatever it is she might be doing— while she's still doing it."

You never know what you're gonna get. Prince's plays host to local politicians, late-night hooligans, and everything inbetween.

Repeat customers, of course, can get so obsessed (especially if they see others sharing their obsession) that they start daydreaming about a place of their own. Over the years the Prince family has seen numerous Hot Chicken outlets open (and just as many close). One of, if not the first, was Bolton's Hot Chicken & Fish, started by former Prince's fry cook Bolton Polk. Nowadays there are a the slew of newer upstarts like Hattie B's, 400 Degrees, Party Fowl, and Pepperfire, as well as dozens of restaurants of all stripes

who offer at least one take on Nashville's now-signature Hot Chicken.

What does Simone think of all the new iterations of Prince's creation? "It depends on when you ask me," she says. "Most of the time I'm like a racehorse. I put my blinders on, and I do what I do. I think there's enough [business] out there for all of us to share. I don't waste a lot of time

thinking about it. I don't go to those places."

She smiles. "I let our customers be the judge. They try the other places and then come back and tell us what they think."

Both Prince women—and let's take a second to note that, despite its man-about-town origins, Prince's today is a product of three strong women (Andre, Simone, and Simone's sister Kim)—say few people ever attempt to steal their secret formula for frying foul . . . but they certainly do ask.

When asked how often she's queried about said formula, Simone Prince sighs, and laughs, a sort of simultaneous emotion that speaks to a joke, once funny, that has morphed into a groaner. "Every single day of my life," she says.

Thinking of taking a gig at Prince's for a few months in an effort to suss out the secret seasonings? You got another think coming there, too.

"Our folks have been with us for a while, most of them," Simone says. "They've probably tried to come up with their own concoction. I'd be lying if I said I didn't have any trouble with 'em, but it's minimal. And they have to sign these confidentiality agreements, so we usually don't have a problem. But I will say this: If they want to fire me up, and in a hurry, they know how to do it."

A DAY IN THE LIFE

It's a balmy Thursday in early September, and Andre Prince Jeffries holds court at her corner booth, as she's prone to do, saying hello to friends both old and new. She informs a love-struck regular that the Prince's security guard the customer has been fancying hadn't turned up yet but will soon. (As it turns out, the guard had left to go vote, with Prince's permission. The woman, dressed to the

 No turning back. Once you get a taste of Hot Chicken, even the the best fried chicken seems to be missing a little something.

★ON THE SIDE★
PICKLED EGGS
The old-timer's favorite is worth a second chance

Pickled eggs are a staple in old-fashioned joints (and not a few dive bars) in the South, and are most often seen in their natural habitat, a big-ass glass jug. Often colored pink, they are something of an acquired taste, but many old-timers still swear by them, and they're making something of a comeback in nouveau-Southern restaurants all across greater Dixie. Once a key ingredient of a workingman's lunch, the pickled egg is still potent, portable, and a delightful conversation starter.

PREPARATION

Place the eggs in sterilized jars. Add vinegar, salt, cloves, mace, allspice, coriander, bay leaves, and sugar to a large saucepan or pot. Bring to a boil. Reduce heat to medium and simmer for five to seven minutes. Pour brine over the eggs. Cap tightly with sterilized lids and rings and process in a hot-water bath for five minutes to seal. After they cool, refrigerate for at least a week before serving. Note: for pink coloration, add pickled beet juice or food coloring.

INGREDIENTS
MAKES 1 DOZEN

- 12 hard-cooked eggs, shelled
- Enough cider vinegar to cover the eggs (white vinegar will suffice)
- 1½ tablespoons salt
- 1 dozen coriander seeds
- 3 bay leaves
- 6 cloves (whole)
- 2 blades mace
- 1 tablespoon sugar
- 10 allspice (whole)

THE PROSELYTIZER

Meet former Nashville Mayor Bill Purcell, Hot Chicken's hype man

If Hot Chicken has a patron saint—or, at least, a saintly patron—it's William Paxson Purcell III. A two-term mayor of Nashville, Purcell supplemented his time in office from 1999 to 2007 with another, not-so-secret part-time job: acting as the world's foremost booster of Nashville's famed signature dish, Hot Chicken.

At the time, Hot Chicken had its proponents; a preparation doesn't attain cult status without a cult, after all, and Hot Chicken's cult had become multi-generational long before Purcell was elected. However, Hot Chicken wasn't really Nashville's signature dish, at least in the popular mind, before Purcell took office and took over head hype-man duties.

What Purcell did do was take Hot Chicken's heat—public perception-wise—and magnify it. He saw to it that folks flying into Nashville could read about Hot Chicken in inflight magazines long before they landed. He held meetings at Hot Chicken restaurants so regularly that folks took to calling Prince's Hot Chicken Shack his "second office." He mentioned it both in profiles and in passing. His crowning achievement came in 2007, his last year in office, when he started the Music City Hot Chicken Festival, a annual greasy get-together that has grown exponentially with each passing year.

Why does he do it? The answer's simple, says Purcell. He loves the spicy stuff.

When did you first try Hot Chicken? What did you take away from the experience?
I first experienced Hot Chicken at Columbo's. Bolton Polk [who later started Bolton's Spicy Chicken & Fish] was the owner and we were his lawyers. They were located at the foot of the Shelby Street Bridge in a building that was later taken by the Arena project. From the first bite of Hot Chicken, I knew life would never be the same. For me it was an immediate reaffirmation of the American Dream. It remains that to this day.

Do you think the Hot Chicken will have staying power?
This is Nashville's indigenous food. There is no question in my mind that, so long as the basic sensibilities of the dish are preserved, Hot Chicken will always be one of the unique American foods—and will always be Nashville's.

How much do you think this uptick in attention might have to do with Nashville's resurgence as a whole?
Nashville's increasing visibility in the world is the result of the things we do right, an important part of which is quality of life—our music, our neighborhoods, and our commitment

to people. Hot Chicken is one critical part of the unique quality of life we share with whoever wants to join us here, for a day or for a lifetime.

You were way ahead of the curve with your vocal support of Hot Chicken. How often do you still eat it?
Once a week is the right dose for all people and all purpos-

THE STATE OF TENNESSEE
HOUSE OF REPRESENTATIVES

BY THE HONORABLE
BILL PURCELL
MAJORITY LEADER

Greetings: Be it hereby known that

Prince's Hot Chicken

in recognition of extraordinary interest in governmental processes and for culinary excellence has been designated

THE BEST RESTAURANT IN TENNESSEE

Given under my hand, this
5th day of November, 1996.

REP. BILL PURCELL
MAJORITY LEADER

es. Should a dose be missed for any reason, it is not advisable to double up.

How did the Hot Chicken Festival go from idea to reality to (now) annual success?
We were to celebrate the 200th anniversary of Nashville's incorporation as a city, the moment in time when our people committed to this place for the long term. The Hot Chicken Festival was the ideal way to conclude that yearlong celebration.

You're known as a proponent of Prince's, but do you visit other Hot Chicken outlets these days? There are certainly more to choose from than when you were in office.
I have tried every known Hot Chicken restaurant in Nashville. They all bring their own special qualities to the dish, but work hard to remain faithful to the basic tenets.

Ms. Jeffries at Prince's speaks quite fondly of you. What's it been like getting to know the family over the years? Have you ever dared to ask her anything about her recipe?
I was at Prince's today and visited with Andre. She is a force of nature and the leading guardian of the process and the product. She is just back from the *Garden & Gun* festival in South Carolina. They served a thousand people last weekend. I expect immigration to increase momentarily.

As Hot Chicken continues to grow in popularity and reach, is there anything that gives you pause?
No. It's all good for us here, and transformative for everyone else.

nines, replies "he better . . . I just got my hair done!") Andre wanders in the kitchen from time to time to keep an eye on things, but generally seems to accept—and thrive in—her role as Hot Chicken's cultural ambassador.

This is typical of Prince's Hot Chicken Shack, America's ground zero for brain-scramblingly scorching fried bird. Andre is asked if she's considering expansion, a rumor that pops up every now and then in Hot Chicken circles like the lively Facebook group, the Fraternal Order of Hot Chicken.

"They always call and tell me what businesses are available, tell me where I might like to move. I just looked at a place that was $10,000 a month. And it was in a strip mall! I like small places, and nothing too big—too much overhead. But $10,000! I said, 'whoo, let me hurry and get back to my little corner of town.' Can you imagine missing a note?"

She then tackles another rumor swirling around the Hot Chicken circuit: that she is soon to be the star of a new reality TV show: "I flew out to Pasadena, California, and met with them and they [the Oprah Network] wanted a Hot Chicken show to air before *Sweetie Pie's*," she says. "I said 'No, thank you.' I don't want no cameras following me around. It's too stressful. Matter of fact, they just called again last week asking me had I changed my mind. I'm not ready for it, bless 'em. I don't imagine I'll ever be."

Andre, who proudly notes that her restaurant doesn't advertise—while leaving unsaid that they don't need to—says

Running the show. Simone Jeffries (left) and Andre Prince Jeffries (right) run the day-to-day business at Prince's.

ANDRE PRINCE JEFFRIES' TOP 10 REASONS WHY PEOPLE ORDER HOT CHICKEN, IN NO PARTICULAR ORDER

1. **It's raining or storming or the power has gone off.** "I don't know why, but the phone rings off the hook."

2. **They need a win.** "When the Tennessee Titans played the Cleveland Browns, the Browns brought their bus down here. They picked up all these whole chickens for the team. Sunday, of course, was the game, and they won!" (Author's note: the 25-point rally is the largest road comeback in the history of the NFL.) "And then the Houston Texans, they came down, got chicken, and they won too. So I'm starting to think that the word needs out that the Titans should come if they care about winning a game!"

3. **They're celebrating a bachelor or bachelorette party.** "And they're keen on acting a fool."

4. **To use as an aphrodisiac.** "Sometimes you see feet hanging out of cars."

5. **Because they saw it on TV or in a magazine.** "'Why you here?' I asked one guy, a TV host. 'This is not weird food,' I said. 'This is not snake eyes or whatever it is. This is not strange food. This is chicken that just happens to be cooked hot.'"

6. **Because they know or are otherwise doing business with former Nashville mayor, Bill Purcell.** "He started the Hot Chicken Festival. He started putting us in the airplanes (in on-board city guides). He's been very influential as far as pushing Hot Chicken is concerned. I give him most of the credit."

7. **Because they're about to give birth.** "A lot of women eat it when they're pregnant, which I don't suggest. At the last Hot Chicken Festival, we had a lady there who ate the medium, and she went into labor! I don't take anything hotter than medium to things like that. But it seemed to have done the trick."

8. **Because their parents fed them hot chicken.** "Kids these days like it hotter than ever before. Maybe they develop a tolerance."

9. **Because they're female.** "They can consistently tolerate it hotter. Men fade much quicker. Somebody should do a study on that."

10. **Because they've been drinking and/or smoking the marijuana.** "This is a late night chicken because it sobers you up. You been out drinking all night long, smoking pot or doing your drugs, it takes you straight off that high. Some people get upset, if they make it here before the police stops 'em, because they say we've blown their high with that Hot Chicken bringing them down."

they are fine with the publicity they receive, as long as it's on the family's terms. They are grateful for it, she says, and even humbled by it, but have never sought after it.

Regardless, it's found them. Everyone from PBS to *The New York Times* to *The Wall Street Journal*—not to mention TV food shows and podcasts too numerous to list here—have alighted here in this little rundown restaurant in a rundown strip mall in a rundown neighborhood on a rundown side of town.

At least, that's how that same media usually describes Prince's native terroir. It's a descriptive that often says more about the reporting outlet itself than it does any particular neighborhood leanings.

NO PLACE LIKE HOME

A *Food Republic* writer once noted the area around Prince's thusly: "After parking your car in the slightly sketchy parking lot in a nefarious neighborhood of North Nashville, you enter through the nondescript front door of the restaurant tucked in-between a nail salon and a hair supplies store in a tiny strip mall. Prince's is open until 4:00 AM on weekends to satisfy the late night cravings of the bravest (and drunkest) of Nashvillagers, but the food is the same during the safer daylight hours."

Choose your heat. The darker the crust, the hotter the bird. At Prince's, even the mild packs a spicy punch.

★ON THE SIDE★
FRIED DILL PICKLES

How do you improve the already perfect pickle? You fry it.

Fried pickles probably aren't the first thing you think of pairing with Hot Chicken, but consider: pickles are a staple side in Hot Chicken joints, and so is fried food like crinkle fries. If you're going to sup on greasy goodness anyway, why not rare back and push all your (pickle) chips in?

PREPARATION

Add the flour and dried spices to a small brown paper bag. Shake to mix. Fill a skillet or dutch oven with two to three inches of oil. Heat the oil to 350°. Drain pickles, then toss in the spice bag. Shake off as much of the excess coating as you can with a sifter or colander. Add the pickles to the oil and fry until golden brown, about four to five minutes. Transfer with a slotted spoon or spatula to paper towels to drain. Serve hot.

INGREDIENTS
4 TO 6 SERVINGS

- 16 ounces dill pickle slices
- 2½ cups all purpose flour
- 2 tablespoons garlic powder
- 2 tablespoons onion powder (optional)
- 2 teaspoons ground cayenne pepper
- 1 tablespoon paprika (smoked or hot)
- 2½ teaspoons kosher salt
- 4 teaspoons black pepper
- oil, for frying (peanut or other high smoking-point oil works best)

★MAINS★
HOTCHICKENIFICATION:
Hot Chicken spice isn't just for chicken anymore

INGREDIENTS

- 3 tablespoons cayenne pepper
- 1½ teaspoons sea salt
- 2 teaspoons dry mustard
- 1 teaspoon sugar
- 1 teaspoon sweet, smoked, or hot paprika
- 1 teaspoon freshly ground black pepper
- ¾ teaspoon garlic powder

In cooking as in music, following a recipe note-for-note can often lead to stilted, seemingly emotionless results. A recipe is like guitar notation or tablature: a guide, a suggestion. The real magic comes when you start playing around with what you have around and improvising. In much the same way that a guitarist might pull out of the air a lick from another style of music seemingly far removed from his own—creating, without even thinking to, something completely new in the process—a true food artist knows there's a difference between the often artificial concept of "fusion"—"the process or result of joining two or more things together to form a single entity," sayeth the dictionary—and real convergence, when two things are drawn to each other almost at a molecular level.

So, you've made the spice mix above, or something like it, and have learned that a little goes a long way. What to do with the rest? Why, get creative! Most anything that likes salt, spice, or heat will take to hotchickenification.

French Fries: Sprinkle a little on as you would a good cajun spice mix or Lowry's seasoning salt. Go with crinkle-cut fries for that true chicken shack vibe.

Popcorn: Again, sprinkle as you might sprinkle salt. If you're also buttering your popcorn, be forewarned that things can get messy in a hurry.

As a Sandwich Sauce: Add a little to your favorite mayonnaise (homemade is best, but if you don't have the time, look for Duke's or Blue Plate for that real Southern flavor).

As a Salad Dressing: Mix ¾ cup of olive oil, four tablespoons good vinegar (red or white wine work well), two tablespoons fresh lemon juice, and one clove garlic, add Hot Chicken seasoning sparingly until ideal blend is achieved. A little fresh bacon grease is a delightful add-in here.

Hot Ketchup: When I was younger, a friend suggested a few good glugs of Tabasco to my Heinz ketchup to perk up fries and the like. Ten years later, they sell spicy ketchup at every grocery in the country. For a smokier, tangier treat than you get off the shelf, use Hot Chicken spice.

Fajita Seasoning: Adds mouth sizzle to a dish that already boasts plenty on the plate.

Remoulade Sauce: A little Hot Chicken seasoning added to remoulade sauce can salve any rich fried seafood dish. Try on a chicken sandwich, fries, or spread liberally on a po-boy.

Ranch Dressing: If you're one of those people who eats ranch dressing on everything, try stirring a little Hot Chicken seasoning in next time around. It won't make up for the myriad condiments you're missing out on due to your Ranch-myopia, but it is a step in the right direction.

Even legendary comedian and TV star Jerry Seinfeld felt the need to comment on Prince's no-frills environs, telling a *Grub Street* interviewer that "It's all black people at, like, two in the morning. It's not in the greatest neighborhood. It was me and two other guys in suits." For this, he was pilloried on Websites like *Gawker* for being alternately out of touch or simply out-and-out racist. (To be fair, Seinfeld also

ended with "I'm definitely going back there, too.")

Andre has heard all the talk, if coded and couched, and doesn't dispute much of it. But she also says that, like with her Hot Chicken, there are things going on under the surface that people could see if they'd stop to take a second and look. "I mean, it does get crazy sometimes," she says. "It has always been a late night place, on Fridays and Saturdays, ever since we first opened. I don't know why they chose to close at four o' clock in the morning, but I have tried to continue the tradition. They say the Grand Ole Opry used to come after their shows on Friday and Saturday and that had something to do with it."

She stares into the parking lot, where a man is trying to park his car in a spot perhaps better suited for a motorcycle.

"We feel safe here," she says, after a pause. "This area is called a 'hood.' I don't know why, but it is. But let me tell you about all my little thugs that I've gotten to know. That's what I call them. They think they're so big and bad, but if they get to know you, and like you, and respect you, as far as the robberies and such are concerned, you're good. But I know it's because of my thugs. They come by to make sure I have some ones, and they come by at close to make sure I get out of here, that I get out of the building and to my car, and pull off. When they have respect for you and know you're not wishy-washy, professing to be one thing while you secretly are another, and they know you are true to your guns, that you're not trying to live undercover. And they do know. They research you. They watch you. It's amazing how they take care of you. And all without you doing anything they're doing, or being in their business . . . whatever it is."

"People always say 'I'm not going to that side of town,'" she continues. "But I know this: If they respect you in your

 Dressed down. Located in a nondesecript strip off an infamous street, Prince's relies on food, not marketing, to keep doors open.

★ON THE SIDE★
TATER SALAD
A better bowl of an old standby to cool the palate

We're not telling you anything you don't already know. Potato salad is delicious, and most who cook it have their own recipe, perhaps one that's been in the family for years. The only real debate with potato salad is whether or not you're in the mayonnaise- or mustard-based camp. Why not step across the aisle and include both next time you're in picnic mode? The mayo in this recipe adds a necessary creamy quality while the tart kick of the yellow mustard serves to keep everything from becoming too cloying.

PREPARATION

Cook whole unpeeled potatoes in a pot of boiling salted water until they are easily pierced with a knife. Drain and peel under cool water and then chop into ½ inch squares. Chop the eggs into large chunks. Transfer potatoes and eggs to a large bowl. Add celery salt, vinegar, mayonnaise, mustard, onion, lemon juice, hot sauce, pickles, bell pepper, celery, and parsley. Mix well, and add more mayonnaise (or a teaspoon or two of olive oil) if the mixture is too dry for your liking. Add salt and pepper to taste. Sprinkle the top of mixture with paprika. Cover, and refrigerate until chilled. Serve cold.

INGREDIENTS
MAKES 4 PINTS

- 5 pounds Yukon Gold potatoes
- 4 hard boiled eggs, peeled
- 2 fresh lemons, juiced
- 1 tablespoon extra-virgin olive oil
- 1½ cups mayonnaise
- ¼ cup yellow mustard
- 1½ teaspoons celery salt
- 2 tablespoons vinegar
- ½ cup finely diced dill pickles
- 2 teaspoons paprika
- ½ cup green bell pepper, chopped
- 3 or 4 stalks celery, chopped
- ½ cup diced Vidalia onion
- Vinegar-based hot sauce to taste
- Diced parsley to taste
- Salt and ground black pepper to taste

neighborhood, they'll make sure you're taken care of. You need neighborhood business, not big business. You need something sturdy, something that's been there for a minute, to help keep a neighborhood together."

THE MYSTERY PERSISTS

Physical history of Prince's origins—and, by extension, Hot Chicken's origins—is scarce. But mystery is abundant. The mystery of the closely-guarded secret ingredients; the mystery woman said to have started the whole Hot Chicken train rolling—eventually reaching destinations as distant as Australia. Also found in great quantities? Rumors and hearsay.

To that end, there is a name and speculation bandied about concerning the identity of Girlfriend X, the woman who supposedly spiked Thornton Prince III's breakfast decades ago. The grand doyenne's surviving family is said to be currently considering its options, perhaps hoping to somehow cash in on their ancestor's (alleged) creation. It's unlikely. Especially given that she isn't around to tell her story.

Until relations thaw, we are left with this: Girlfriend X is said to have passed on none other than July 4—the same extra-hot day that Nashville celebrates its annual Hot Chicken Festival (for more on the Hot Chicken Festival, see pages 68-69). If, as some say, coincidence is the messenger of truth, this could be seen as particularly significant sign.

However, if you're like most people, the mystery—the mysteries—behind Hot Chicken are a fun diversion, but they are really only that: Something that serves to fan the flame of our fandom, not the source of the heat itself. The core of good Hot Chicken, both literally and figuratively, has always been, and must always be, the chicken. It's the first and only rule, really. And it's been the same way since the very beginning.

If you've can make room. Top off an already gluttonous meal with sweet relief from one of Prince's pies.

THE JOINT
Prince's Hot Chicken Shack: The Enduring Original

PRINCE'S HOT CHICKEN SHACK

Location: 123 Ewing Dr. #3, Nashville, Tennessee 37207

Phone: (615) 226-9442

Web: None (They do have a Facebook page, but don't expect regular updates.)

Heat Levels: Plain, Mild, Medium, Hot, Extra-Hot. Considered the gold standard of Hot Chicken joints, other places even base their temperature scale on Prince's—i.e., "our 'Hot' is a Prince's 'Medium.'" Speaking of which, an order of Prince's Medium is usually plenty hot for most, but real pepperheads seeking a transcendent experience might opt for the Hot. (Only sadists and the suicidal go for the Extra-Hot.)

Sides: Baked beans, potato salad, slaw, and pickles. Many eschew sides altogether, excepting perhaps the pickles. Order plenty of pickles.

Don't Miss: You're going to Prince's for the chicken, and, who's kidding who, the experience . . . everything else takes a back seat. All the chicken is fried to order, so block out a couple hours of time just to be safe; Prince's is not the kind of place you go for a quick workaday lunch, unless you're a freelancer. Like your chicken boneless? Then don't miss Chicken Tender Thursdays, the only time Andre Prince Jeffries and Co. roll out the kid-friendly foodstuff. (Unless you want Child Services to pay you a visit, make sure you order the wee ones Plain or Mild.)

CHAPTER TWO
(HOT) CHICKEN OR THE EGG?
A PREPARATION HEATS UP

Let's take as a given that Prince's Hot Chicken Shack (or, at the very least, Thornton Prince III and his female friend) invented the preparation we now know as Hot Chicken. And why not? There's never been a single theory or origin story proffered to refute the account. And nearly everyone concedes that the family was first with a Hot Chicken restaurant in Nashville. ➡

That's not to say that everyone agrees on the details of said tale, however. A person cannot be sure if a ubiquitous telling means that it's somehow more true and authentic, or simply more oft-repeated. There are so many stories, in fact, that even the Prince family doesn't agree on many of the details among themselves. What's more, there's no "smoking gun" to be found: say, an earlier recipe, film, photograph, or the like.

As such, it could be said—and has been said—that all of these Hot-Chicken-Joint-come-latelies have "stolen" Prince's signature dish, if not their recipe. On some level, of course, this is true. To look at it another way, if certain dishes aren't copied or replicated or repeated on other menus across town, they could never become truly popular in the first place. If someone doesn't take the Prince's idea for Hot Chicken and try their hand at their very own take, you're

not reading pop-culture paeans from the likes of The Black Keys' Dan Auerbach, and you're certainly not reading this book right now. If something's going to begin locally and travel globally, people must first like it enough to rip it off.

HOT CHICKEN FLIES THE COOP

There are many Hot Chicken restaurants amongst us now—in Nashville, nationwide, and abroad—and over the years there have been even more that have tried and failed, or at least closed. It's worth pointing out that the continued growth and success of Hot Chicken joints means that there is a huge demand for the stuff.

Prince's has been tormenting tongues since pop music meant Bing Crosby instead of Beyoncé. And there are now

No Frills. A small walk-up window, a few indoor tables, and a few tables outside make up Bolton's, one of the early, enduring joints.

WHITE BREAD AND PICKLES
A primer on Hot Chicken essentials

Many places that serve Hot Chicken do so along with pillowy slices of white bread and a brace of pickles.

They're decidedly not side items, these two. Both are included free with your order at any reputable purveyor, and are as much of the overall experience of eating Hot Chicken as the bird itself. But why? And how did this come to be?

We'll look first at the white bread.

First, it's cheap. And it's plentiful. When you're putting out hundreds of orders a day, fresh-baked Sourdough isn't the most financially-sound option. There's white bread for sale at convenience marts, for crying out loud. And as anyone knows, it's uber-cheap. A good rule of thumb for home Hot Chicken aficionados is to never go over two dollars a loaf. You'd think a higher-end bread would be better, but you'd be wrong. (The June, 2014 issue of *Bon Appétit* recommended that you "Do like locals: Serve the chicken atop sliced soft white bread." Note how that implies you're used to regularly slicing your own.)

The white bread also makes a great blank canvas for the bright slashes of color to come. It's the most opaque edible possible: It's literally "square," and relatively tasteless. It's as unobtrusive as food gets—even the name, "white bread," suggests blandness. As such, it is the perfect foil for the true star of the show.

Lastly, the bread does a wonderful job of soaking up some of the spice mixture that will inevitably drip down the freshly-fried—and if it ain't freshly fried, run—Hot Chicken. When you begin eating your Hot Chicken, you'll find yourself tearing off little pieces of bread here and there in an effort to quell the flaming *flagrante delicto* taking place on your tongue. Ten or so minutes in, all you're likely to have left is a bright red, gummy, grease-soaked, chicken-shaped wafer, which has now nearly bonded to your chicken. Some fans are adamant that this is the best part of the meal.

As to where the pickles came from, who knows? They do seem to help temper the heat, albeit in measurable-in-millisecond increments. The relief offered is akin to drinking a thimbleful of cold water after some torturous trek: welcomed, but with no backup in sight, almost a tease. Sturdy, affordable pickle chips like those made by Mt. Olive work well, and are cheap besides. Which, again, is something of the point. It is a supporting actor playing a bit part—you want the pickle to do well, but not overshadow the name on the marquee.

One last tip—most places will let you order extra pickles and white bread as a side, even as you'll receive a generous portion with your order. Be forewarned, however, that a few longtime Hot Chickeneers may look at you, smirk affixed to their grill, confident in their belief that you're merely delaying the inevitable.

They may be right. But everyone's got his or her own way of eating Hot Chicken, which is part of the fun. It's going to linger with you for a while, so why not take your time with it?

numerous new-school Hot Chicken purveyors—Hattie B's, Hot Stuff Chicken & Fish, 400 Degrees, and Pepperfire among them—who boast their own loyal supporters who prefer the new iterations of Hot Chicken over the original.

So how did we get here? What happened to all the years in between? Truth is, not a lot of people know.

The Lost Years of Hot Chicken—which we'll say lasted from 1950 through 2005—weren't well documented. The best we might hope, given this lack of evidence, is a sort

Hot Chicken steps it up. Once a cult food with a few fans eating from a handful of places, Hot Chicken now comes with decor.

of generally acknowledged timeline. What's now known as Prince's Hot Chicken Shack is usually given credit as being first—although a few old-timers speak of a place called Bo's being around at roughly the same time.

Later came Columbo's (which helped birth Bolton's Spicy Chicken & Fish), and Pee Wee's Place, owned by the legendary Nashville restaurateur and raconteur Pee Wee Johnson. There were other spots, too, all of which, at the very least, counted Hot Chicken as a signature dish: places like Mr. Boo's, Dixie's, hotchickens.com, Wilma Kaye's, Emerial's, and Joe's HOTTTT Chicken. Most didn't make it.

One, rather notably, did make it. Bolton's Hot Chicken & Fish, a Main Street mainstay in East Nashville, started life as The Chicken Shack in the 1980s. The Chicken Shack was an immediate success. Impressive, especially when you realize that their signature dish was still a hyper-local delicacy, and there was no tourist-padding the lunch numbers.

The restaurant closed after a few years, as patriarch (and onetime Prince's employee) Bolton Polk's health began a slow decline. But before Polk passed away, he gave an inheritance of sorts to his nephew, Bolton Matthews: He bequeathed Bolton his recipe for Hot Chicken.

Bolton Matthews and partner Dolly Ingram had heretofore run successful, separate janitorial businesses. After months of discussion, they decided to take some of that good clean money and open Bolton's Spicy Chicken & Fish. The "& Fish" was Dolly's idea, as she'd enjoyed notoriety of her own for her particular take on fried seafood.

As a slight aside, Ingram's alternate theory of Hot Chicken's genesis—which she shared with Southern Foodways Alliance's Amy C. Evans back in 2008—is that the preparation might have its roots in an older generation accustomed

The Second Gen. Using a passed down recipe, Bolton's roadside shack has been run by Bolton Mathews and Dolly Ingram for years.

EVERYTHING YOU EVER WANTED TO KNOW ABOUT CULINARY HEAT BUT WERE AFRAID TO ASK

A brief chat with legendary food scientist Harold McGee

You'll be hard-pressed to find a professional kitchen that doesn't boast at least one well-worn copy of Harold McGee's classic *On Food & Cooking: The Science & Lore of the Kitchen*—it continues to be the go-to text for understanding the science behind cooking. But McGee's work is also instructive for the home cook. (Find Harold McGee online at curiouscook.com.) Following is a chat with McGee on the science of spice.

Is there a point at which our taste buds can stop registering heat? Is there a hot so hot that you couldn't register anything hotter?

All of our sensory systems can be overwhelmed by a stimulus and fail to register further increases, and I imagine that the same is true of pungency.

A lot of places marinate their chicken overnight in buttermilk with a bottle or three of hot sauce poured into it. Is there any chance that any of that heat gets in the chicken from the marinade? Or is it perhaps maybe more for show/a tradition, as some suggest?

The pungent molecule capsaicin is large and doesn't easily penetrate tissues, so overnight marination would spice up only the surface.

Is the endorphin release from eating something like Hot Chicken (or anything really hot) actually "addictive" in any way?

The general idea of food addiction is controversial among psychologists, and I've found no report of any actual study of the addictiveness of pungency.

TASTE, ON TOUR
Joe Kwon of The Avett Brothers

Joe Kwon's day job is cellist for The Avett Brothers. When he's between sets, however, he likes to explore whatever town he happens to be in, taking in that burg's food culture. Although he'll occasionally end up at a white tablecloth place like Per Se or Fearrington House, he usually tends towards more economical eats.

"When I think of Nashville, I think of young talented chefs with a vision for food that is accessible and delicious...and of course hot chicken," Kwon says. For more tips both Nashville and nationwide, visit him at tasteontour.com.

When did you first try Hot Chicken?
I first tried hot chicken not long after Hattie B's opened up in Nashville. I walked in thinking I could take the heat... and walked out humbled.

Is it something you eat on a regular basis? Is it a food that could have staying power, do you think?
I'd say as long as the chicken is good without the heat, then yes, it has staying power. People love fried chicken, and the heat to some is an added bonus. Regarding the extremely hot stuff, I believe there will always be the brave souls generation after generation who will try to stomach the heat.

Other than the health effects of eating a lot of fried chicken, I can't see any downside (to its continued popularity). Maybe the biggest downside, if there is one, would be the heat not translating well over the Tennessee border and "Hot Chicken" slowly being mainstreamed into "peppery chicken" for the sake of fulfilling more palates.

I think that if you enjoy Hot Chicken it's not a gimmick or a stunt food. I personally love hot chicken, but the next time I go get Hot Chicken I'll be having the medium!

to using hot peppers in place of salt, the better to avoid exasercating their hypertension, an affliction especially prevalent in the African American community at the time. This idea, which Ingram suggested as a possible theory, nothing more, is not without merit, if unprovable. But then again, to date, such is the Prince's "revenge" narrative.

The building Bolton and Dolly settled on can best be described as sort of a lowboy shotgun shack, with minimal seating indoors and a table or two outside, depending on the weather. The "sign," as it were, is painted on the building, quite colorfully, along with a phone number, some cartoon chickens and fish, and a bulletpoint listing of their most popular side items: "SLAW—BAK BEANS—POT SALAD."

The Heat is On. Aqui Simpson, owner of 400 Degrees, cooks what many Hot Chicken afficonados consider Nashville's spiciest bird.

NASHVILLE JOINTS BRING THE HEAT

Thankfully, it's easier to trace the line from Prince's and Bolton's to the newer kids on the block than it is to recreate the origin story with any certainty.

While it doesn't have the history of Prince's or even Bolton's, 400 Degrees—started in 2007 by Nashville native

★MAINS★
HATTIE B'S "MEDIUM" HOT CHICKEN
All the spice and a new twist on taste

INGREDIENTS

- Two 3½–4-lb. chickens, each cut into 10 pieces (breasts halved)
- 1 tablespoon freshly ground black pepper
- 2 tablespoons plus 4 teaspoons kosher salt
- 4 large eggs
- 2 cups buttermilk or whole milk
- 2 tablespoons vinegar-based hot sauce (such as Tabasco or Texas Pete)
- 4 cups all-purpose flour
- Vegetable oil (for frying; about 10 cups)
- 6 tablespoons cayenne pepper
- 2 tablespoons dark brown sugar
- 1 teaspoon chili powder
- 1 teaspoon garlic powder
- 1 teaspoon paprika
- White bread and sliced pickles (for serving)

Hattie B's is not the oldest Hot Chicken restaurant in Nashville—that'd be Prince's—nor does it serve the hottest, according to most Hot Chicken-heads (Prince's or 400 Degrees, most seem to agree). What it does boast is a great flavor profile, as well as a remarkable consistency, two things that are often forgotten by some of the Johnny-come-lately joints. Hattie B's does offer two incendiary flavor levels—"Damn Hot" and "Shut the Cluck Up"— but lots of folks swear by the medium, which is probably the best entry point for a beginner. Again, no Hot Chicken joint is going to give you their exact recipe, but this one, from the restaurant's head chef John Lasater, is probably as close as you're going to get without applying for a job there/signing a confidentiality agreement.

PREPARATION

Toss chicken with black pepper and 2 tablespoons of salt in a large bowl. Cover and chill at least 3 hours (or, better yet, overnight). Whisk eggs, buttermilk, and hot sauce in a large bowl. Whisk flour and remaining 4 teaspoons of salt in another large bowl. Fit a Dutch oven with thermometer; pour in oil to measure 2 inches. Heat over medium-high heat until thermometer registers 325°. Pat chicken dry. Working with 1 piece at a time, dredge in flour mixture, shaking off excess, then dip in buttermilk mixture, letting excess drip back into bowl. Dredge again in flour mixture and place on a baking sheet.

Working in 4 batches and returning oil to 325° between batches, fry chicken, turning occasionally, until skin is deep golden brown and crisp and an instant-read thermometer inserted into thickest part of pieces registers 160° for white meat and 165° for dark, 15–18 minutes. Transfer to a clean wire rack set inside a baking sheet. Let oil cool slightly. Whisk cayenne, brown sugar, chili powder, garlic powder, and paprika in a medium bowl; carefully whisk in 1 cup frying oil. Brush fried chicken with spicy oil. Serve with bread and pickles.

and Tennessee State University grad Aqui Simpson—certainly has its adherents. Some folks think 400 Degrees' version of Hot Chicken is the city's fiery-est, and Simpson has drawn acclaim for another spicy contribution to "Nashville Hot" foods, too: the Hot Pork Chop.

Located on Peabody Street at the Corner of 4th Avenue in a nondescript brick building that houses Quizno's and locally-owned Nuvo Burrito, 400 Degrees offers a unique heat-level approximator: 100° is code for mild; 200° for medium; 400° gets you "hot." Other heat levels exist, if you know to ask for them—and 600° teeters between the limits of human consumption and masochism.

Despite less than a decade in the business, Simpson's restuarant has had an effect on the Hot Chicken scene as a whole. Many of Nashville's newest Hot Chicken entrepreneurs cite 400 Degrees as a formative influence (and/or addiction), including Isaac Beard of Pepperfire.

To have lasted as long as Simpson has making Hot Chicken in Nashville, you have to be doing something right. And indeed she is. How do we know this? She's still in business. As is the case with very little else in Nashville,

Hot Chicken refines the aesthetic. Spots like Hattie B's (below) and Pepperfire (left) tweak the look of the chicken shack.

★ON THE SIDE★
HATTIE B'S BLACK-EYED PEA SALAD
A cold salad with a tasty tang

INGREDIENTS
PEPPER VINAIGRETTE:

- ¼ cup champagne vinegar
- ¼ cup malt vinegar
- ½ cup extra virgin olive oil
- ½ teaspoon fresh thyme (minced)
- ½ teaspoon fresh parsley (finely chopped)
- 1½ teaspoons freshly-ground black pepper
- 1 teaspoon fine sea salt (plus more to taste)
- 1 red bell pepper (small dice)
- 1 green bell pepper (small dice)
- 1 yellow bell pepper (small dice)
- 2 scallions (finely sliced)
- ½ teaspoon fresh roasted garlic (minced)

BLACK-EYED PEAS:

- 2 cups dried black-eyed peas
- 4 strips of bacon
- 6 cups chicken stock or vegetable stock

Black-eyed peas are the epitome of earthy-tasting goodness. Which is not to suggest that they taste like dirt, but rather that they contain some sort of slightly-bitter toothiness that tastes like warm comfort to many. The addition of diced bell peppers, tangy vinegars, and fresh herbs, as seen in this recipe courtesy of John Lasater of Nashville's Hattie B's, makes this Southern comfort food come alive for anyone. It's crunchy, bitter, mushy and tangy all at once, and is the perfect foil for that restaurant's "Damn Hot" or "Shut The Cluck Up" Hot Chicken.

PREPARATION

Start by making the vinaigrette. Whisk together the vinegars, olive oil, thyme, parsley, black pepper, half the salt, all the bell peppers, scallions, and garlic. Let sit overnight.

In a large pot, add enough water to cover the peas by about 3–4 inches. Do this the same time you make the vinaigrette, because they have to soak overnight. Drain peas in a colander and set aside. In a large pot over medium-high heat, render the bacon, leaving it whole so it is easy to remove when finished cooking. Once bacon is rendered, add all the chicken stock and bring to a simmer.

Once simmering, add the peas and cook on low for about 25 minutes. You want them to be tender, but not mushy. Strain the peas and remove the strips of bacon. While the peas are hot, toss in the vinaigrette and add ½ teaspoon of salt and any additional salt if needed. Chill and serve.

there is consensus on what to do with Hot Chicken restaurants that fake the funk: Avoid them, their cafeteria-size cans of hot sauce, and pre-fab powders until they get the picture and quietly slink away, never to be heard from again.

HOT CHICKEN FOR THE MASSES

Adding Hot Chicken to your restaurant's menu is clearly an enticing proposition for a restaurateur, especially in Middle Tennessee. There are a few foods that adherents refer to in language—"I'm addicted! I gotta get my fix!"—usually reserved for more illicit activities. And how many foods boast a built-in fanbase so rabid that they form online societies like the The Fraternal Order of Hot Chicken?

Humble beginnings. The Original Pepperfire (left) was a small walk-up window that later grew a porch and a dedicated following.

Two successful new-school Hot Chicken establishments, Pepperfire Hot Chicken (2010) and Hattie B's Hot Chicken (2012), credit their survival to not forgetting the food's roots, both culturally and culinarily.

"Advertising 'Hot Chicken' will get people in the door," says Isaac Beard of Pepperfire, located on Nashville's well-traveled Gallatin Road. "At the same time, it's a genre of cooking people are kind of obsessed with. You certainly want to put your own stamp on it, but you have to offer them quality—every time. It's up to you to keep them coming back."

Beard says that while he ate (and *eats*, "every day of the week, except Sunday and Monday, when most of us are closed") Hot Chicken for years before starting his own place, the solutions didn't come easily. In fact, he says he spent three years perfecting his current proprietary spice blend only by "eating a lot of bad chicken along the way."

"We didn't know what to expect when we finally opened," Beard says. "My wife and I knew Aqui (Simpson) from 400 Degrees, and she told us that when she opened her first location, she was there what seemed like six months before anyone ever walked through the door. When we opened up, we were packed. I don't know if it was the area we're in, or all the social media stuff we did beforehand, but we were off to the races pretty fast."

After he had his spice blend down, Beard began looking at the Hot Chicken business itself.

"Of all the Hot Chicken restaurants that lasted, we figured out they had some things in common," Beard says. "They had to be within lunchtime driving distance from downtown (Nashville), and they had to be within walking distance of the local community. We sort of didn't follow that, but we took a chance on our feeling that East Nashville was about to hit."

MAYOR KARL DEAN
Nashville Mayor continues his predecessors' love of Hot Chicken

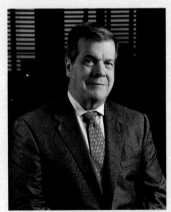

Two term Nashville Mayor Karl Dean isn't as vocal as his mayoral predecessor Bill Purcell in his love of Hot Chicken, but he, like any good politician, knows the value of an iconic food to a region—think Chicago without deep-dish pizza or Boston without clam chowder . . . if you can—even as he makes a point to emphasize our ever-expanding dining options start, rather than end, there.

"The first time I tried hot fried chicken was at Prince's over lunch with then-mayor Bill Purcell," Dean says. "I was the city's Law Director at the time. Since then, I've attended the Music City Hot Chicken Festival annually and have judged the amateur cooking contest every year I've been mayor. It's one of the highlights of my summer.

"I don't naturally gravitate to spicy food, but I like Hot Chicken because it's more than just a meal—it's an event. Talking about how much heat is packed in the chicken—and how much water or sweet tea you need to drink to cool down—can be as much fun as eating it. While Hot Chicken certainly doesn't define Nashville's food offerings by itself, it has helped put our great city on the culinary map. And we'll always take another serving of that."

ON SECRET INGREDIENTS

"Whatever hysteria exists is inflamed by mystery, suspicion and secrecy. Hard and exact facts will cool it."—Elia Kazan

One of the main things Hot Chicken has going for it is that it's cloaked equally in mystery as it is hot pepper paste. The Hot Chicken origin story is clouded in intrigue, and indeed its very preparation is most often proprietary to the establishment serving it. While every Hot Chicken recipe likely sticks to some very basic ingredients—chicken, oil, cayenne, garlic and/or onion powder—each establishment usually has a few ingredients or techniques they keep close to the vest (or apron, as the case may be). Following, we try to tease out a few of these secret substitutions. Which isn't to say they are all in use—but it's not to say they aren't, either.

Paprika (smoked or hot variety) A little smoked paprika (or the hot variety of same) provides a certain umami to Hot Chicken while not overpowering it, serving as a middle layer of sorts, and boasting both bitterness and depth. What's more, it's wonderful for helping achieve that bullfighter's-cape red color that makes Hot Chicken so iconic and, well, beautiful.

Acidity (vinegar, pickle juice) So, what kinds of things do Hot Chicken joints go through on a regular basis? There's chicken, of course, and cayenne, and there's certainly no shortage of white bread making it's way through the door of any Hot Chicken shack—consider that your average place goes through a loaf every 10-12 customers.

What else? Pickles. Gobs and gobs of dill pickles. And when you go through countless quarts of pickles on a daily basis, what does this leave you with? Why, countless quarts of unused pickle juice. Pickle juice is an excellent tenderizer and marinade, as well as a vinegar replacement. So why use a different acid when you've got gallons of the stuff just sitting there looking for a use?

Pork Fat (lard, bacon, or otherwise rendered pork fat) Some Hot Chicken places still use lard, which is by very definition processed pork fat, instead of oil. However, many places, especially the ones who don't pan fry their chicken,

use oil. A little lard in the spice mix, however, imparts a certain savory quality to chicken. The effect doubles if you use a little rendered pork fat (in this case, bacon drippings). Is it cheating? A crutch? Maybe. But many of the homestyle Southern dishes we all love best have pork as a seasoning. Why should Hot Chicken be any different? If you do decide to go in the lard direction, here are a few thoughts to squelch your guilt: Lard has less saturated fat, more unsaturated fat, and less cholesterol than an equal amount of butter by weight, according to Herbert W. Ockerman's *Source Book For Food Scientists*.

Sugar Sugar is a natural pairing with searing heat. It not only helps calm the mouth (or so say its proponents), it also helps lend a depth to hot foods (or any food), according to Harold McGee's *On Food and Cooking: The Science and Lore of the Kitchen*: "Sweetness helps mask both sourness and bitterness from other ingredients. And flavor chemists have shown that it has a strong enhancing effect on our perception of food aromas, perhaps by signaling the brain that the food is a good energy source and therefore deserves special attention." As Hot Chicken can be both strongly acidic and/or bitter, depending on the preparation, a little sugar, judiciously added, can help provide a certain evenness to hot foods. See other famous sweet/hot pairings such as chocolate with chilies, certain Mexican moles, pad thai, and indeed many Eastern-inspired pairings like sweet chili sauces and chutneys.

Beard, an avid Hot Chicken historian—he owns all manner of Hot Chicken memorabilia, including numerous pieces of original Music City Hot Chicken Festival poster art—focused much of his attention on Prince's, where he says he still dines often.

"They've gotten pretty comfortable in their position," Beard says of Prince's. "And why not? I think a lot of people underestimate Ms. Jeffries. My suspicion is that, despite what her media persona may be, she's flat out brilliant. If you could examine the way she thinks, I think there's a good chance that she's a genius. The way she's kept that business going, and thriving, is brilliant. She's built a massive restaurant. You don't luck your way into that kind of success."

Beard says that all of the Hot Chicken purveyors he knows are at least publicly cordial with one another, and

In the Beginning. Simple picnic tables on a covered porch made up the dining room of the original Pepperfire.

most are happy to suggest to their customers other Hot Chicken places to try, noting that each has their own selling points. Hot Chicken is such, he says, that people will usually gravitate toward a favorite after a while, but still will support the greater enterprise as a whole.

"Most of the old Hot Chicken places, it was a family thing. The further you try to get away from that, I think you start to lose something," he says. "It's one of the special things about Hot Chicken. It's like sports—you cheer, if you will, for your favorite Hot Chicken place. You'll eat at all of them—just like you'll watch any team play if you're bored—but you usually have a rooting interest."

Beard's first experience with Hot Chicken was not unlike many folks'—incomprehension at first, followed by undeniable compulsion.

"My friends kept telling me I needed to try Hot Chicken," he says. "I went to Prince's, since it was the oldest. Stood in line, ordered my food, checked it off the list. It wasn't bad, but also not the most amazing thing I'd ever eaten. Then, about a month later, late at night, I woke up and all I wanted in life was some Hot Chicken. And from that moment on, I was licked. I crave it. There's something legitimate there in Hot Chicken that's not there with say, Buffalo wings. I'm sure there are people out there who can't go without Buffalo wings. But it's a sauce. It's not real spice. There are some people who can give or take Hot Chicken. But then there are some people who, it just grabs them inside-out. It's legitimate heat, legitimate spice."

Beard remembers one story well. "I was eating down at 400 Degrees one time and this lady was sitting near me and we were both eating our chicken. At one point she leans over and whispers 'I'm addicted.' She said it in a way like she didn't want anyone to know, or overhear. Like it was sinful. She sensed a fellow addict."

The new Pepperfire. Pepperfire moved just down Gallatin Road to a refinesd space that still retains that funky Hot Chicken vibe.

SWEET, SWEET HEAT
Talking Hot Chicken with Andrew Zimmern

Half a dozen years or so ago, if you mentioned the name Andrew Zimmern to someone outside the culinary world, you'd be greeted with a blank stare.

"Andrew Zimmern," you'd continue. "You know—the guy with that show on the Travel Channel? Eats mongoose eyeballs and the digestive tracts of water moccasins and such?"

At this point, most usually knew who you were talking about. Since the early success of that show, *Bizarre Foods with Andrew Zimmern*, the ever-enthusiastic Minnesotan has grown into an iconic figure in the world of food media. (Zimmern received prestigious James Beard Foundation awards for *Bizarre* in both 2010 and 2013.) People tuned in for the icky foodstuffs and left, consciously or not, with a greater understanding for the nooks and crannies of cultures heretofore alien to us, whether found abroad or across the street. That show's success soon led to *Bizarre Foods America* and *Andrew Zimmern's Bizarre World*.

These days, he balances copious TV work with speaking engagements and writing for magazines. He's also produced two well-received books, *The Bizarre Truth: How I Walked Out the Door Mouth First . . . and Came Back Shaking My Head*, a collection of essays, and *Andrew Zimmern's Field Guide to Exceptionally Weird, Wild, and Wonderful Foods*.

Mostly, of course, he does what he always has: he travels, he researches, he eats, and he thinks about it, humbly suggesting that we'd do well to do the same.

Following, he considers Nashville's own bizarre bird, Hot Chicken.

You spoke at the 2014 Music City Food + Wine Festival on Hot Chicken. What drew you to that topic?

If you're going to do a demo and presentation in Nashville, why not go all out and "take the coals to Newcastle," as it were? I was talking some about the history of Hot Chicken, my Hot Chicken experiences, and my food demo (was focused) on spicy chicken dishes from other parts of the world—with the prescription that if you're in Nashville, and you want Hot Chicken, you're probably overlooking a-whole-nother way to approach it.

What is it about the pairing of chicken and spice that works so well together?

I think they're ideally suited for one another. You don't need to have a high-fat food like pork belly to make something spicy. I think chicken and chilies have an affinity for each other. I'm a big Chinese food junkie, and you see it lots of other cultures too: Malaysian, African . . . it's a relatively common pairing.

What would you say to those who might try to marginalize Hot Chicken by deeming it a "stunt food"?

I think whoever calls it a stunt food is ignorant of the point. This is not gimmick fare. This is not a scorpion you get inside a lollipop at the museum gift shop. This is a way of eating. There are numerous restaurants in Nashville, dozens and dozens and dozens. Think of a restaurant like Husk, a "table-cloth" newcomer that does a version of it. Catbird Seat did their version of it. You know, Hot Chicken is as much a part of the city as a New York City pizza or hot dog is to that town. So you have hundreds of versions of it, everybody does theirs, and the Hot Chicken houses all have their level of spice to which the customer can choose from. I don't think it's a stunt food at all. Spicy food hits a receptor button in our pleasure center that either you like, and you keep hitting the button back, or you don't! People love spicy food in America. Again, I think chilies and chicken are actually born for each other. I don't see that anything "stunt" about it. Just look at two of the more famous ones like Prince's and Hattie B's. You know, that's exquisitely cooked chicken.

What was your first introduction to Hot Chicken?

I went to the city and I went to Prince's. I then had the opportunity to eat Hot Chicken when it was cooked by Nashvillians outside of Nashville at food festivals and such. And then when I went down and did my show in Nashville about a year ago, I had a different version every single day. I had a Hot Ramen at Otaku South. I had the Hot Chicken course at Catbird Seat. I went to Hattie B's. I went to Prince's again. And then I went to like four or five others, like little bars who happened to serve Hot Chicken along with, you know, some kind of sandwich lunch special. The crew each day ate it too, and so you had a good barometer with which to tell the story of it. There's not a fast food place in the country that doesn't have a spicy chicken sandwich. People have to be reminded that Hot Chicken is not just hot. It's something different than that.

Is it possible that the exponentially-expanding food media behemoth has fed the popular rise of Hot Chicken?

I think you hit the nail on the head. Americans since the time of DeToqueville have wanted to see images and pictures of themselves. You have a rapacious, underfed food media out there, throwing up stories at a pace at which that is unprecedented in any other time. We are excessively hungry for different stories to tell. Nashville has a very deep and widening culture, there's the intersection of music and food there. It's a famous Southern town with a great history, it has a booming tourism capacity, and the minute that the food freaks started to get a little traction down there, it was just a matter of time before this is the next big thing. And sure enough, three or four years later, there it was. Hot Chicken isn't the reason that we went down to Nashville for our show, but I can tell you that when we decided to go to Nashville to do a show, it was the first idea that went up on the board. Again, I don't know if its chicken or the egg (laughs) but I can tell you that all of those reasons are the sum totality of why it's taken off. I really do think that the biggest thing is that we have this starving atmosphere for new stories. So everyone is churning the ground looking for these things. So it was only a matter of time.

HOT CHICKEN SPREADS LIKE WILDFIRE

Nick Bishop Jr., co-owner and operator of Hattie B's Hot Chicken, knows his way around a kitchen. His father, Nick Sr., runs Bishop's Meat & Three in Franklin, Tennessee., and his grandfather, Ernest Eugene "Gene" Bishop, was a cafeteria counter worker who worked his way up to eventually taking the reins as CEO of Morrison's, the cafeteria and dine-in restaurant giant.

It was at Bishop's Meat & Three that the seed of what would later become Hattie B's was first planted.

"I was in the music business [at John Prine's Oh Boy Records] for about seven years," says Bishop. "After hanging

The family business. As part of a line of successful restaurateurs, Nick Bishop Jr.'s Hattie B's drew crowds from day one.

that up, I just thought I'd help my dad run Bishop's. He still believed in that way of eating and cooking. At some point, he started getting back into Hot Chicken. We'd taste it from wherever he happened to go on that given day, and one day we happened upon a recipe that we decided had to be similar to the base spice blend that everyone uses.

"And so, we began tweaking it. One day we might add smoked paprika. The next day it might be Kosher sea salt. We finally found a version we liked, and we put it on the menu at Bishop's to see how it would do. Eventually, it became about 30 to 35% of our entree sales, and that's when we said 'You know what? We might have something here.'"

To say they "have something" is an understatement. Since opening the Midtown location in 2012, the restaurant has been namedropped repeatedly in magazine and newspapers, enjoyed hours on food TV, and, in late 2014, saw its head chef, John Lasater, make the *Forbes* "30 Under 30" list at about the same time the Bishops opened a second Hattie B's off of Nashville's up-and-coming Charlotte Pike.

Success brings a new set of challenges, Bishop says.

"We might well be people's first Hot Chicken experience when they come to town, based on what they've read somewhere or what they've seen on TV. We really have to knock it out of the park every day. We want to be a good representative, not only of our brand, but of Hot Chicken in general. You can learn about Hot Chicken here, but we'll tell you, 'Hey, go try Bolton's. Go try Prince's. Go try Pepperfire or 400 Degrees.'"

"I like think we've been good caretakers of the legacy of Hot Chicken. The recipe we give to *Bon Appetit* or a cookbook? That's not our real recipe. And honestly, it's not that I even really care. It's part of the game, and everybody else does it. So we're like, okay, we'll play along. That's sort of what's fun about it. The mystery adds to the experience.

CAN'T GET ENOUGH?

Competitive eater Molly Schuyler, the world's Hot Chicken Champ

Molly Schuyler is a two-time winner of the Franklin American Mortgage Music City Bowl World Hot Chicken Eating Championship. She polished off 4.3 pounds of the stuff in 8 minutes to win the 2013 Championship, and a mind-boggling 4.75 pounds to take the 2014 title, the latter victory completing an undefeated "season" of eating. A wisecracking, married mother of four who tips the scales at a mere 120 pounds, Schuyler says spicy eating competitions are always tricky, but for really putting a body through hell, nothing beats Nashville-style Hot Chicken.

"Wow! That stuff is hot!" Schuyler says. "I had never eaten spicy chicken of this magnitude before. My first bites were not so bad. You could tell there was spice, but as you eat in a contest, without a chance to recover, the pain builds intensely. I could not have prepared for what I had to eat. I actually really do like very spicy food, just not when I have to eat it fast and in quantity. The chicken would have been just stellar with a side of ranch!

"Although I love spicy chicken," she says, "this is the most painful of all the contests I have done—both during and after. I was still feeling the joy three days later. Many bathrooms thank me. I can't wait to come back next year, though! Bring it on!"

★MAINS★
CARLA HALL'S HOT FRIED CHICKEN
Celebrity chef celebrates her Nashville roots

INGREDIENTS

HOT BRINE:

1 quart water

¼ cup habanero hot
sauce, or other very
spicy hot sauce

¼ cup Kosher salt

¼ cup sugar

8 boneless, skin-on
chicken thighs

FRIED CHICKEN:

- ¼ cup canola oil, plus
  more for frying
- 1 tablespoon cayenne
  pepper
- ½ teapsoon sweet
  paprika
- ¼ teaspoon garlic
  powder
- ½ teaspoon sugar
- 1½ teaspoons Kosher
  salt, divided
- 2 cups flour
- 1 teaspoon freshly
  ground pepper

Carla Hall's Southern Kitchen in Brooklyn is the famed chef and TV personality's first-ever restaurant, and she's made Nashville-style Hot Chicken that eatery's *raison d'être*. If that doesn't speak to the expansion of Hot Chicken, nothing will. Granted, the *Top Chef* and *The Chew* star was raised in Nashville—which only adds to her Hot Chicken bonafides— but such a name casting her lot with what was heretofore seen as a regional dish is nonetheless an aggressive bet on the food's staying power outside of Nashville. Over a quarter of a million dollars in Kickstarter funding would seem to suggest that the market is there. While Hall has never had a namesake restaurant before, her shrewd business acumen would seem to suggest a success. (Recipe courtesy of Carla Hall.)

PREPARATION

To brine chicken: In a large bowl, whisk water, hot sauce, salt, and sugar until sugar dissolves. Submerge chicken in liquid and refrigerate at least 1 hour and up to 6 hours.

To prepare fried chicken: Heat ¼ cup oil in a small saucepan over medium heat until shimmering. Add cayenne, paprika, garlic powder, sugar, and 1 teaspoon salt. Cook, stirring, until fragrant, about 30 seconds. Transfer to a small bowl and reserve.

In a large resealable plastic bag or a paper bag, combine the flour with remaining ½ teaspoon salt and 1 teasspoon black pepper. Add chicken in batches and shake well until all pieces are evenly coated. Add enough oil to a cast-iron or other heavy skillet to reach ½ inch up sides. Heat oil over medium heat until it reaches 365°. The oil's ready when a little flour dropped in bubbles and sizzles steadily. Remove chicken from flour, shaking off any excess. Carefully place a few pieces of chicken in oil, skin side down. You don't want to crowd pan. Keep adjusting heat to keep a steady sizzle and to maintain oil at 365°. Cook until browned on bottom, about 3 minutes, then carefully flip each piece. Cook until browned on bottom, about 3 minutes. Then continue cooking and turning to evenly brown until cooked through, about 10 minutes total. Crumple up some paper towels and drain the chicken on them. Repeat with remaining chicken, replenishing and reheating oil between batches. Transfer chicken to a serving dish and drizzle with reserved spice oil. Serve hot.

THE TEN COMMANDMENTS OF HOT CHICKEN

1. Thou shalt not touch thy eyes with thy fingers after eating Hot Chicken.

2. Thou shalt know that this goeth doubly for touching other sensitive areas, on yourself or others.

3. Thou shalt wear rubber gloves when preparing Hot Chicken in a home setting.

4. When mixing the spices, consider wearing a mask like you've seen on doctors and Michael Jackson, to avoid the inevitable violent cayenne-dust sneezing fits.

5. Practice the patience of Job. Which is to say, thou shalt not be in any sort of hurry as regards any aspect of Hot Chicken. It was slow food before Slow Food was cool.

6. Seriously. Don't touch your eyes, even if you just used a wet-wipe to clean your fingers.

7. Do not order the "Extra" Hot anywhere, least of all at the iconic Prince's, a.k.a. the Garden of Heat-en.

8. Do not expect any Hot Chicken accountrements—white bread, pickles, sides, drinks—to in any way lessen the pain. You don't set out to eat Hot Chicken not expecting—not craving—the heat.

9. Do not visit Nashville, eat real Hot Chicken, and then start a restaurant serving a toned-down, tepid version in hopes of Bringing Hot Chicken To The Masses.

10. Lather, Rinse, Repeat.

But all the components—the garlic, the paprika, the cayenne—they're all there. If I say cayenne's the base of our Hot Chicken blend, I'm not giving anything away, you know?"

Bishop says that the best one can hope for in the Hot Chicken business is a level of consistency in the finished product. On some days, this means more work than on others. "Heat is a very inexact science." he says. "Maybe your peppers aren't as hot for a couple of days because of some weather anomaly. Maybe your supplier changed one of his subcontractors. All these things can cause your heat to fluctuate. What we did with our recipe was try to round out the flavor, where you have the heat, but also have the sweet and the savory that maybe you don't get everywhere.

"That said, I think we're all somewhat the same," he continues. "I don't think we're as hot as Prince's or Bolton's. I mean, we can burn your head off if you want, but we have a lot of people that come in to just get regular old Southern fried chicken, too. And we're happy to serve it to them. We want to serve young people, and their grandmothers."

Some of those loyal customers—although, as of yet, no grandmothers—have even gotten to see the world from the other side of the always-bustling Hattie B's lunch counter.

"As we've grown and become more of a name, people seek us out to a certain degree," Bishop says. "We have people who were weekly Hattie B's eaters who now work here. They saw that we have fun and serve good food and it's a low-stress place, and wanted to work here. Which is great. You don't have to teach them to speak to your brand or the food—they were already doing it."

Bishop often references "The Brand" in conversation, but never in an overarching, Roger Goodell-like fashion. To Bishop, "The Brand" is more about an idealized version of what Hattie B's both is and can be.

In 2014, Hattie B's hired the former General Manager

★ON THE SIDE★
PICKLED OKRA
The perfect pickle isn't a cucumber at all

If you're over a certain age and live in the South, you've eaten a multitude of pickled options over the years—and that's not counting cucumbers. Pickled eggs are commonly sighted and served, as are Vienna-like sausages and pigs' feet. These delicacies are sold in large plastic jugs, the pickling brine pleasingly (or putridly, depending on your tastes) tinted pink. One easy way to move past pickles is to make pickled okra. It's a great use for excess produce, and the pickling process neutralizes okra's notorious penchant for sliminess. What's more, they're absolutely delicious and easy to make. They're also, hands down, the finest garnish for a Bloody Mary. Recipe courtesy Eliza Brown.

INGREDIENTS
MAKES 4 PINTS

- 2 pounds medium-size okra pods
- 1-2 handfuls of dill
- 4 garlic cloves
- 3 cups water
- 1 cup white vinegar
- ¼ cup salt
- pinch of powdered alum

PREPARATION

Wash and trim okra, and soak in ice water for 24 hours. Drain well. Sterilize your pint jars. Bring vinegar, water, salt and alum to a boil, stirring well. Slowly boil for 10-15 minutes uncovered. Put a sprig of dill and one garlic clove in each jar. Pack okra into the jars, alternating ends of the okra. Pour hot solution over the okra in each jar leaving ½ inch headspace. Let sit for one hour, or until solution stops bubbling. Refill each jar as necessary. Cap tightly with sterilized lids and rings and process in a hot-water bath for five minutes to seal.

LET US NOW PRAISE FAMOUS HEN
Nashville's Annual Hot Chicken Festival

About the only thing hotter than Nashville-style Hot Chicken is Hot Chicken as it's served at the Music City Hot Chicken Festival.

Held annually at Nashville's East Park on July 4, the chicken served at the Hot Chicken festival is usually no more incendiary than your everyday "medium," but in tandem with a humid Southern summer, somehow seems twice that.

Designed as a celebration of all things Hot Chicken, this scorcher of a soirée offers free Hot Chicken samples (provided by the likes of Prince's Hot Chicken Shack, Bolton's Spicy Chicken & Fish, 400 Degrees, Pepperfire, Hattie B's

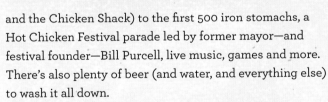

and the Chicken Shack) to the first 500 iron stomachs, a Hot Chicken Festival parade led by former mayor—and festival founder—Bill Purcell, live music, games and more. There's also plenty of beer (and water, and everything else) to wash it all down.

Gaining traction by the year is the amateur cooking contest, where six pre-selected folks (or teams, such as 2013 winners Atomic Yardbirds, with their brilliant "Love us today/Hate us tomorrow" banner branding) compete for the title.

For more information, go to www.hot-chicken.com.

from Pinewood Social and Marché, two esteemed Nashville dining spots, and then hired John Lasater (from well respected spots like Flyte and Porter Road Butcher) to be their executive chef and cooking show representative.

"We're growing, and we're continuing to grow," he says. "But I don't want to lose the focus that's served us so well up to now. Would we like 100 stores? Sure. You want your business to be successful. But it has to work, and that's a feel thing. If it expands outside of (Middle Tennessee), say if we went to Louisville or Birmingham or wherever, we'd want it to be a reflection of Nashville Hot Chicken. But, for it to work, it also needs to be a reflection of their city. We'd talk to them about having their own local beers on tap, and

pulling from the resources that makes their city special. And that includes the human element."

The human element is something both Bishop and Beard enthusiastically insist is as equally important to Hot Chicken as anything up to and including the cayenne pepper.

"One thing all the successful Hot Chicken places have in common is the family element," Bishop says. "It can be the kind you have with your blood relatives, and certainly there's your family of employees, and there's another kind too—the kind you form with the people who come to eat your food."

A new face. On culinary up-and-coming shortlists of all ilk, John Lasater is Hattie B's executive chef and lead ambassador.

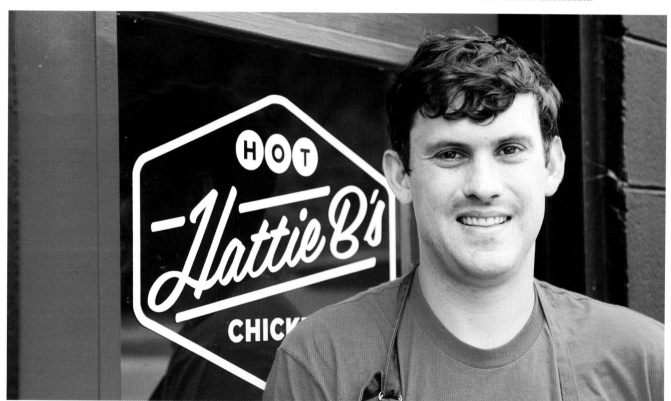

THE JOINTS

Nashville hot spots carry a torch for hot chicken

BOLTON'S SPICY CHICKEN & FISH

Location: 624 Main Street/Nashville, Tennessee 37206
2309 Franklin Pike/Nashville, Tennessee 37204
Phone: (615) 678-4794 / (615) 712-7137
Web: www.boltonsspicy.com
Heat Levels: Spice levels are generally acknowledged to be slightly tamer than Prince's; they also use a drier spice coating than most other Hot Chicken establishments.
Sides: Pinto beans, mac 'n' cheese, turnip greens, green beans, baked beans, french fries, potato salad, spaghetti, corn on the cob, mashed potatoes, slaw
Don't Miss: Don't hesitate to pick up a fish sandwich (whiting, grouper, catfish, or tilapia) while sating your Hot Chicken fix. And the pinto beans—and, when available, white beans—are also a good bet, as are turnip greens.

HATTIE B'S HOT CHICKEN

Location: 112 19th Ave. South/Nashville, Tennessee 37203
5209 Charlotte Ave., Nashville, Tennessee 37209
Phone: (615) 678-4794 / (615) 712-7137
Web: www.hattieb.com
Heat Levels: From Southern (standard lightly seasoned fried chicken) to Mild to Medium to Hot to Damn Hot to Shut The Cluck Up.
Sides: Greens, french fries, pimento mac 'n' cheese, baked beans, redskin potato salad, cole slaw, black-eyed pea salad
Don't Miss: In town for a weekend visit and have a hankering for some Hot Chicken on a Sunday? Hattie B's has you covered. Along with Pepperfire, they also boast the most-convenient take-out of the bunch, meaning you'll still wait a little bit, but where you choose to do said waiting is up to you. The pimento mac 'n' cheese and black-eyed pea salad are justifiably famous (and don't forget that the recipes for both are on pages 24 and 53).

400 DEGREES

Location: 319 Peabody St., Nashville, Tennessee 37210

Phone: (615) 244-4467

Web: www.400degreeshotchicken.com

Heat Levels: 0° (no spice), 100° (mild), 200° (medium) 400° (hot), and various 100 degree increments henceforth if you request kindly.

Sides: Baked beans, potato salad, cole slaw, french fries

Don't Miss: The fried pork chop sandwich is gigantic, and surprisingly tasty, but, as with Prince's, the chicken is still the thing here—try the 400°, which is undeniably hot, but not maniacally so.

HELEN'S HOT CHICKEN

Location: 1222 Rosa L. Parks Ave., Nashville/1801 Jefferson St., Suite 101 (Otey Plaza), Nashville, Tennessee 37208

Phone: (615) 484-7460 / (615) 964-7331

Web: helenshotchicken.com

Heat Levels: Plain, Mild, Hot, Hella

Sides: French fries, baked beans, potato salad, pickles

Don't Miss: Helen's Hot Chicken and Waffles, served with syrup and butter. Helen's—named after Helen Mallard, the Nashville soul-food icon behind the now-defunct Helen and John's—also serves wings, but go for the meatier cuts.

PEPPERFIRE HOT CHICKEN

Location: 1000 Gallatin Avenue/Nashville, Tennessee

Phone: (615) 582-4824

Web: pepperfirehotchicken.com

Heat Levels: Southernfied (plain), Light Mild, Mild, Medium, Hot, X-Hot, XX-Hot

Sides: Collard greens, fried okra, mac 'n' cheese, red potato salad, baked beans, french fries

Don't Miss: The Tender Royale (a deep-fried pepperjack cheese sandwich topped with three chicken tenders), or the AppleJack, which is the Tender Royale topped with sweet apples.

CHAPTER THREE

WONDER BREAD TO WHITE LINEN

HOT CHICKEN LEAVES THE ROOST (AND, IN SOME CASES, TOWN)

We're in the middle of a Hot Chicken renaissance. In recent years, not only have myriad traditional Hot Chicken shacks popped up in Middle Tennessee, countless others have sprouted all over the United States and beyond. Hot Chicken has also gone highbrow, with top-shelf deconstructions and reimaginings by a wide variety of bold and creative chefs. ➡

If in recent years you've picked up a magazine, clicked on a blog, or listened to a podcast, you've probably heard or read a feature about Nashville. From media monoliths like *The New York Times, Rolling Stone,* and *Bon Appétit* to a slew of smaller outlets, there have been countless mentions of Nashville recently, almost all of them overwhelmingly positive in tone.

If you happen to live in Nashville, you may have responded to yet another "It City" piece by rolling your eyes or seeing dollar signs. If you live *outside* of Nashville, you probably default to a mental picture of all the bearded and braces-bedecked hipsters you imagine live here. (Spoiler alert: They do. Mind you, Nashville doesn't have the market cornered on lithesome lasses wearing Harry Carey glasses and dudes in deerskin, unless you ignore Brooklyn, Portland, or the National Basketball Association.)

But Nashville also has it's share of mothers and fathers and soccer coaches and hairdressers and garbagemen and tax attorneys and Aldi clerks and short order cooks and all of the other people you meet wherever and whenever people gather together in the spirit of community.

This fact does not necessarily make for sexy copy. What makes a place great to live is not always what makes for a great story. What makes a community work, on the other hand, is the *intangibles*, which are hard to list, being as they are, by definition, *not tangible*.

Many Nashvillians like the attention the city has received over the last couple of years. With only a few caveats, we want these new people here. We marvel at the cool new restaurants, bars, and boutiques sprinkled in places once

Hot Chicken hits the road. Nashville's unique take on chicken is now a draw in hot spots from Ohio to Australia. ➡

Q&A: STEVEN SATTERFIELD

Famed Atlanta chef on the growing interest in Hot Chicken

Atlanta's Miller Union is a restaurant simultaneously forward-thinking and old-fashioned. If you've ever met its executive chef, Steven Satterfield, this will come as no surprise. His dishes, tasty and tasteful, are most often super-seasonal, produce-centric takes on regional favorites.

Despite Miller Union's placement on the "Best New Restaurants in America" lists from *Bon Appétit* and *Esquire,* not to mention his own 2013 and 2014 James Beard Foundation Best Chef: Southeast nominations, Satterfield's not one to spend much time chasing down guest judge spots on food TV, preferring to spend his time on the ground—see work with Slow Food Atlanta, Georgia Organics and the Southern Foodways Alliance for starters—or digging his hands *into* the ground, in search of the freshest vegetables available.

He's not above the occasional grease feast, however, as he shares below.

When did you first try Hot Chicken? What did you take away from the experience?
I went to a Southern Foodways Alliance-sponsored field trip to Nashville and tried Prince's Hot Chicken for the first time. I immediately fell in love.

Hot Chicken is hotter than ever, and is beginning to dot menus country—if not worldwide. The concept has translated well—but do you think the food itself will have staying power?
I think everyone likes fried chicken, and people who like spicy food can be fanatical about it. This is one of those universal dishes that appeals to spicy food lovers (across the board). And all of the warnings people give you make it a fun game your first time around—"don't touch your face," "wash your hands well before you pee," "you will feel high," that sort of thing.

How much do you think this popularity might have to do with Nashville's own resurgence over the past few years?
There's no question about it, Nashville is *hot* right now. Any Southern city that has a decent food scene and a signature style is going to be showing up on other people's radars soon enough.

Are there any downsides to a food becoming trendy?
My only concern is the quality of the bird itself. I'm a huge proponent of pastured poultry in response to the factory-farmed birds that are so cheap and prevalent in the US. I would challenge a chef to do a sustainable Hot Chicken!

earmarked for Hair Worlds or purveyors of title loans. More people means more money to spend. And if more money is spent, more money goes back into our local economy.

How does this relate to Hot Chicken, you may ask?

Simple. When something small, regional, and fun begins to take off—or when the flattering soft light of media attention begins to shine upon it—weird things happen.

It begins like this: a thing—a place-specific thing—radiates on some level and seems comfortable in its own skin. Then someone visiting from another place encounters this thing and decides he wants to take this thing back with him to share it with *his* place. Think of the first sailor who brought a Muddy Waters or Blind Lemon Jefferson record to Liverpool or North London. Think of how such a thing can sometimes be feted in its new environs, perhaps with a passion that even people from where the thing is *from* can't muster or understand. Those where the thing is from, after all, are used to the thing and don't see it as a big deal anymore (or perhaps never did). Think about how these blues records, to continue the example, led to things that no one could ever foresee: heavy rock, for one. Also, The Rolling Stones. Eric Clapton. Led Zeppelin. Swinging England. Britpop. Cool Britannia.

The same type of thing happens with food. Most every thing we eat in the United States has its origins elsewhere, if we're willing to trace it back far enough. But this hasn't stopped potatoes and tomatoes from being popular here, or—on a more macro level—tacos, salsa, pizza, or french fries. If something's intrinsically *good*, it stands to reason, it stands a chance.

Other foods, for whatever reason, never catch on, becoming, in a sense, the Flavor of the Month. Often, this is not the foods' fault: As Andrew Zimmern noted on pages 60-61, the food media machine is bigger now than at any time in recorded history, and its thirst for content—ever-*regenerating* content—is positively unslakable.

All of that said, few Nashvillians wring their hands about Hot Chicken's increased national presence. But it might sting a little bit. To continue the musical analogy, consider the *I saw 'em in a smoke-filled room with four other people before they SOLD OUT and GOT BIG* mentality that can

Sticking to tradition. Some, like Hot Chicken Takeover in Columbus, Ohio, serve straight up Hot Chicken in keeping with tradition.

★MAINS★
HOT TEMPEH
Nashville restaurateurs tag-team a vegetarian version

INGREDIENTS
SANDWICH

- 2 slices wheat bread, lightly toasted
- avocado, cut into strips
- lettuce (iceberg will do in a pinch)
- sliced tomato
- shredded carrots
- bean sprouts
- Veganaise, or other vegan mayo
- tempeh steaks (The Wild Cow marinates theirs)

THE RUB

- ⅓ to ½ cup hot frying oil or other fat source (to replace Hot Chicken's lard)
- 3 tablespoons cayenne pepper
- 1 tablespoon light brown sugar
- Sea salt and freshly ground black pepper
- ½ teaspoon paprika, smoked or hot
- ½ teaspoon garlic powder

After being made aware of my interest in Nashville-style Hot Chicken, I've had countless friends tell me that they want nothing more but to try a piece of the fiery foul, but that doing so would effectively put the kibosh on their vegetarian/vegan lifestyle. I'm sympathetic to their plight. Mind you, I'm nothing approaching a vegetarian, but I also don't consider a meatless meal to be "missing" something. Sometimes I make the meatless version of a given dish, and sometimes I don't. I like meat, but like the writer Mark Bittman, I prefer it more for its flavor and umami than its heft or size, and believe that the less meat we eat, the better for our health, our pocketbook, and the environment.

Which brings us back to Hot Chicken. What's the best and most notable thing about Hot Chicken? The "Hot." The Hot in Hot Chicken invariably comes from a spice paste. If the paste is the thing, the thinking goes, why hasn't someone come out with a vegetarian Hot "Chicken" experience?

Our prayers have been answered. In an exceedingly rare cross-restaurant collaboration, two Nashville chefs, The Wild Cow's Nick Davis and Pepperfire Hot Chicken's Isaac Beard, teamed up to create two different "Hot Tempeh" dishes: A take on the Cow's signature beans-and-greens, and a toasted sandwich so well-balanced and, well, tasty that you'll want to add it to your Nashville-style "Hot" repertoire regardless of your meat leanings.

PREPARATION

Bake tempeh according to instructions on package (you're looking for it to have a slight, fried-chicken-like crisp on the outside, yet still tender and chewy throughout). Assemble rub mix, brush liberally on tempeh. Toast bread. Spread both sides with Veganaise. From the bottom up, layer lettuce, tempeh, lettuce, carrot, avocado, tomato, and sprouts. Assemble sandwich, slice diagonally, toothpick each triangle.

★MAINS★
CORNISH GAME HENS, HOT CHICKEN-STYLE
A delicate dish with bold spice

There was an ubiquitous commercial for A.1. Steak Sauce that aired often back in the 1980s. In it, a tow-headed kid is aghast that his uncle is putting A.1. on his hamburger. The uncle answers: "My dear nephew, what is hamburger—chopped ham? No! It's chopped steak. And what's better on steak than . . . A.1.?" This anecdote is shared because you might get some looks serving up Cornish game hens dressed in Hot Chicken seasoning instead of lemon and herbs. If so, channel your inner Uncle A.1.: My dear, what are game hens, but little tiny chickens? And what goes better on chicken than . . .?

PREPARATION

To spatchcock the Cornish hens, use poultry shears or kitchen scissors to remove the hen's spine. Then press down on the breast bone to open it out flat.

Pat hens dry. Rub with a little of the olive oil and as much of the spice mix as you feel you're up to. Then let sit for 20 mins at room temperature. Heat a large skillet with the oil over medium-high heat. Add hens, skin side down, to skillet. Top hens with another pot, dutch oven, or other flat, weighty kitchen implement (in a pinch, use a brick wrapped in a kitchen towel). Cook until juices run clear in thickest part of hen and the thickest part of the thigh reaches 165°—about 15 minutes a side. For added heat and to help crisp the skin, mix spice mix with olive oil and reapply to the skin about 5 minutes before the bird is done.

INGREDIENTS
SERVES 4

- 2 Cornish game hens
- 2 teaspoons black pepper
- 1 teaspoon white pepper
- 1 tablespoon Kosher salt
- 2 tablespoons cayenne pepper
- 2 teaspoons dark brown sugar
- 1 teaspoon dry mustard
- 1 teaspoon chili powder
- 2 teaspoons garlic powder
- 2 teaspoons smoked paprika

★ON THE SIDE★
GRILLED BEETS
Yes, they are good for something besides pickling

INGREDIENTS
FOR THE BEETS

- 5 pounds red beets
- ½ cup extra virgin olive oil
- ½ cup apple cider vinegar
- 3 tablespoons shallots

FOR THE YOGURT

- 16 ounces Greek yogurt
- 1 preserved lemon, skin only, minced
- 1 tablespoon salt
- 1 tablespoon black pepper, freshly cracked

Most folks who say they hate beets have probably only tried the pickled variety you often see in all-you-can-eat salad bars at nondescript steakhouse chains. They're blood-red and limpid, and don't taste like anything more than the pickling juice in which they're served. Real slow-roasted beets—or grilled, as in the recipe below—are often a revelation to folks who've previously disdained the ruddy root vegetable. A splash of a simple vinaigrette takes them from sumptuous to sublime.

PREPARATION

Coat the beets evenly with all ingredients. Roast in a baking dish, covered with foil, at 350° for approximately 90 minutes, or until the tip of a knife pierces the beats with ease. Remove from the oven and use a hand towel to help peel the beets. Then cut them into wedges. Strain the liquid from the pan and reserve for later.

For the yogurt, mince the skin of 1 preserved lemon and mix with one large container of greek yogurt, 1 tablespoon of salt and 1 tablespoon of fresh cracked black pepper.

To serve, toss beets in canola oil and season with salt, then grill sliced beets on a hot grill. Remove when heated through with nice grill marks, and toss with sliced chives, minced shallot and reserved roasting juices. Serve over preserved lemon yogurt.

become too common. But there's pride, too. Mostly, Nashvillians just hope that the carpetbagger types don't screw it up for everybody. Perhaps some hope they *do* screw it up, so the local version comes home to roost where it damn well belongs.

THEIR FIRST BITES

All of the folks mentioned in this chapter have one thing in common: They first experienced Hot Chicken in its home habitat, and were suitably inspired to create their own take on Hot Chicken.

Some, like ramen shop Otaku South's Sarah Gavigan, use their native specialty as a starting point for a culinary journey. In Nashville restaurants alone, you'll also find high-end foodie versions like The Catbird Seat's Hot Chicken Skin topped with "Wonder Bread" puree, and the Pepperfire/The Wild Cow vegetarian mashups: a Hot Tempeh sandwich and a "beans and greens" salad with garlic aioli.

Others strive to be as faithful to the original recipe as possible—or their *idea* of what an original recipe is, because, as discussed, ain't no one giving you their *actual* Hot Chicken recipe.

"I first tried hot chicken in 2008 in Nashville," says Jared Van Camp, executive chef at Chicago's Leghorn Chicken. "And what I remember most is how numb my mouth was. I was working at Blackbird in Chicago at the time, and we listened to Yo La Tengo all the time in the kitchen—their song, 'Return to Hot Chicken,' is what inspired me to try Hot Chicken and first put it on my radar."

Van Camp—who estimates he eats Hot Chicken four or five times a week—says the reason he helped start Leghorn was to sate a "hot tooth" that he developed after eating in Nashville.

"When we started in Chicago, there wasn't anywhere to

DON'T GET ABOVE YOUR RAISIN'

A quick reminder from Damon Lee Fowler on the dangers of being anointed the next (next) big thing

Damon Lee Fowler, a founding member of the Southern Foodways Alliance and a revered voice on all things Southern cooking, cautions that popularity can come with its own set of risks. "There is always a downside to a particular food becoming trendy," he says. "All too often it means that a perfectly good, respectable dish is 'reinvented' practically beyond recognition, dumbed-down as it travels further and further from its place of origin, and frequently overshadows other dishes from the same region/place that might be superior to it (shrimp and grits in the Lowcountry is one good example of this)."

★MAINS★
HOT CHICKEN SALAD
When Buffalo meets Nashville, interesting things happen

INGREDIENTS

- 4 hot chicken tenders (recipe below)
- 2 cups mixed baby greens
- 4 celery sticks
- 4 carrot ribbons
- 3 tablespoons bleu cheese crumbles
- 4 dill pickle chips, julienned
- 3 ounces. bleu cheese dressing (recipe below)
- Chives for garnish

HOT CHICKEN TENDERS

- 4 chicken tenders
- 2 cups all-purpose flour
- 2 cups panko bread crumbs
- 2 tablespoons hot spice mixture (recipe below)
- ½ cup canola oil

SPICE MIXTURE

- 2 tablespoons cayenne pepper
- ½ teaspoon paprika
- 1½ teaspoons granulated garlic
- 2 teaspoons salt
- ½ teaspoon black pepper

BLUE CHEESE DRESSING :

- 1 ½ quarts Hellman's Mayonnaise
- 1 cup onion, minced
- ½ teaspoon garlic, minced
- ½ cup parsley, chopped
- 2 quarts sour cream
- ¼ cup lemon juice
- 10 oz. blue cheese, crumbled
- 1½ teaspoons salt
- 1 teaspoon white pepper
- ½ teaspoon cayenne pepper
- ¼ cup tarragon vinegar

This salad from The Southern Steak & Oyster is a collaboration between TomKats Hospitality Group owner Tom Morales and Executive Chef Matt Farley, and draws inspiration from the spicy chicken Chef Farley grew up eating in the Northeast—Buffalo chicken. Hence the combination of celery, carrots, and bleu cheese wih the quintessential "Nashville" Hot Chicken accoutrement—pickles.

PREPARATION

Toss the greens with 2 oz. of bleu cheese dressing in salad bowl. Place carrots and celery on top of greens. Place chicken tenders then top with 1 oz. of bleu cheese dressing, bleu cheese crumbles, pickles, and then garnish with chives.

For the tenders, combine all ingredients in a large bowl. After you have made the breading, mix the rest of the spice mixture with ½ cup of canola oil and set aside. Bread and fry the chicken tenders. When tenders are fully cooked, pass them through the oil and spice mixture. Set aside until ready to build the salad.

To make the spice mixture, combine all ingredients in a small bowl.

In another bowl, combine all ingredients for the blue cheese dressing, stirring the crumbled blue cheese in last.

HUGH ACHESON

A brief chat with the forthright Georgia chef

Hugh Acheson is living proof you don't have to be born in the South to cook its food. The 2012 co-winner of the James Beard Foundation's Best Chef: Southeast, Acheson was born in Ottawa, Ontario, Canada. After moving to Athens, Georgia, with his wife (and a brief stint as Sous Chef under Gary Danko at the latter's Restaurant Gary Danko), Acheson opened Five & Ten in Athens in 2000. By 2002, he was named as one of *Food & Wine's* Best New Chefs. In 2007, he opened The National, also in Athens, and in 2010, he opened the acclaimed Empire State South in Atlanta. Also the possessor of a much-commented-upon unibrow no less worthy than that of New Orleans Pelican superstar Anthony Davis, Acheson's accolades are many: his *A New Turn in the South: Southern Flavors Reinvented for Your Kitchen* won the 2012 James Beard Foundation award for "Best Cookbook in American Cooking," and he was the co-winner of the Foundation's 2012 Best Chef: Southeast award, sharing the honor with Linton Hopkins (see pages 112-113).

Whenever he's in Nashville, Acheson says he makes it a point to nab some Hot Chicken, usually at Prince's Hot Chicken Shack. Like Matthew McConaughey in those infamous Lincoln ads, he says he doesn't do it to be cool, or to make a statement. He just likes it.

When did you first try Hot Chicken? What did you take away from the experience?
The first Hot Chicken experience I had was at Prince's in Nashville. It was medium, which translates to HOT AS HELL.

Do you think Hot Chicken has staying power? For instance, it's a dish which instantly precludes anyone with an aversion to spice/heat from even trying it.
Thai food can be a four alarm deal. And Sichuan. I think it has staying power, but in toned-down form. Eating the equivalent of a tablespoon of cayenne in a meal will not be widely accepted or have sea legs. Make it buttery, and tone it down. Then we got a winner.

How much do you think this upwardly mobile export might have to do with Nashville's resurgence as a whole over the last five years or so?
A little bit. But not a lot. Nashville has grown up culinarily due to people giving a fuck. That is a national trend in midsized cities.

Are there any downsides to such a food becoming trendy?
Yeah, look at kale. We work hard to get people to eat better, kale takes hold and gets some attention, and then gets a backlash? It's a green vegetable . . . save your anger.

get Nashville-style chicken, so opening our own place was kind of selfishly motivated—so we could have it ourselves."

Van Camp doesn't believe that something becoming more commonly *available* necessarily leads to a more homogenized or "common" result. "American palates have really grown," he notes. "Their tastes have gotten less regional and more evolved. Even people with an aversion to spice are more open to trying new things these days.

"I think it's great that Hot Chicken has kind of taken off and is starting to garner more media attention," Van Camp says. "Like anything, the more people that are exposed to it, the more the good places stand out. It educates people, so I see it as a benefit."

Chicago's own. Jared Van Camp of Leghorn Chicken says he started selling Hot Chicken, in part, to satisfy his own cravings.

★MAINS★
OTAKU SOUTH'S HOT CHICKEN BUNS
A patently Asian take on a wholly Southern dish

INGREDIENTS
9 SERVINGS

- 3 boneless, skinless chicken breasts
- 2 cups buttermilk
- 3 cups white vinegar
- Kosher salt
- 1½ tablespoons sugar
- 1 small bunch fresh dill
- Black pepper
- 2 teaspoons whole coriander
- ½ teaspoon ground turmeric
- 1 medium cucumber
- 2½ tablespoons dark brown sugar
- 2 tablespoons sweet paprika
- 1½ tablespoons ground guajillo chile
- 1½ tablespoons ground habanero chile
- 1½ tablespoons cayenne pepper
- 1 cup all-purpose flour
- 1 cup potato starch
- Bao buns
- 6 cups canola oil

FOR THE SLAW

- 2½ cups shredded cabbage
- ¼ cup Kewpie mayonnaise

Sarah Gavigan of Nashville's Otaku South is one of the many cooks and chefs taking the core ingredients of Hot Chicken—the chicken, the bread, the pickles—and deconstructing them and reimagining them into new and exciting forms. Here, she takes a boneless breast, fries it, and adds a few Japanese-cum-Kentucky touches, and serves the whole thing on a steamed white-bread bao bun with Kewpie slaw.

PREPARATION

One day ahead: Cut the breasts into nine pieces as close to equal rectangulars as possible. In a nonreactive bowl let them marinade overnight with the buttermilk.

One day ahead: Bring the vinegar, salt, black pepper, sugar, dill, coriander, and turmeric to a boil. Meanwhile, slice the cucumber into ¼-inch slices and put them in a casserole dish. Pour the vinegar mixture over the cucumbers. Allow it to cool, then weight down the cucumbers with a plate and transfer the dish to the fridge.

The next day, make the Hot Chicken spice by combining the brown sugar, paprika, guajillo, habanero, and cayenne. In a wide shallow bowl, prepare the mixture for dredging the chicken by combining the flour and potato starch. Add salt and pepper to taste. If you're using a bamboo steamer, add water to your wok and make sure the steam is rolling when you add the Bao buns. They take about 7 minutes to steam from frozen, but they will hold in the steamer for up to 15 minutes.

In a skillet, heat the oil to 350°. Pull the chicken from the buttermilk and allow it to drain. Dredge the pieces in the flour mixture and fry until floating, 3 to 4 minutes, or until golden brown. Transfer them to a paper-towel lined plate. Add a touch of the frying oil to the Hot Chicken spice and toss the fried chicken pieces in the spice. Just before serving, prepare the slaw by combining the cabbage and mayonnaise with a touch of salt and pepper. Assemble the bun by layering the chicken first, then add the pickles and top with the slaw. Close the bun and serve.

Most Asian markets carry Kewpie mayonnaise, boa buns, and bamboo steamers.

HOT OR NOT?

Sussing out what is (and isn't) Hot Chicken

Is the chicken boneless?

Verdict: HOT, although as with #2, people will argue this point. While most enthusiasts will argue Hot Chicken tastes better off the bone, fried chicken tenders are still fried chicken, and fried chicken, doused with the proper seasonings, is Hot Chicken.

Is it anything other than fried?

Verdict: NOT. Hot Chicken is hot fried chicken, as enumerated above.

Has it been stored, at any point, under a heat lamp?

Verdict: NOT. As Tom Petty knows, the waiting is the hardest part. And the anticipation that's making you late, that's keeping you waiting? Even Carly Simon knows that hunger makes the best sauce.

It says right there on the menu: "Nashville-style." It's got to be righteous Hot Chicken then, right?

Verdict: Certainly not the case. There are already restaurants in other states (Texas, we're looking at you) who've violated multiple of the above in the name of "Nashville-style," but then again, copying Nashville is how we got Austin.

Is the chicken finished in any way with bottled hot sauce?

Verdict: NOT. Hot sauce is only permissible during the marination stage.

Is it served with anything other than white bread, either atop the bread or between two slices of it?

Verdict: HOT, but with caveats: It's still Hot Chicken, but not the classic Hot Chicken experience longtime acolytes crave. Which is not to say that the Hot Chicken and waffles that a place like Nashville's Pepperfire serves isn't a delicious dish (and surefire brunch-picker-upper) in its own right.

HOT CHICKEN CROSSES THE ROAD

At the core of the Big Apple Hot Chicken movement—Carla Hall's eponymous new Southern Kitchen notwithstanding—is Brooklyn/Bed-Stuy's Peaches HotHouse. Co-founder Ben Grossman says he and his partner Craig Samuel first heard about the fire-bird from Samuel's wife, Laura Canty-Samuel.

"Laura is a professional actor, and she often traveled with her company," Grossman says. "During one of her trips, she heard about this amazing Nashville staple. She asked around, and was led to Prince's, that strip-malled, faded-paint-window-signed, vinyl-table-cloth-covered, fluorescent-lit 20-seat temple of its own creation."

"A couple of weeks later, Craig and I took a trip to Nashville and tried Prince's, Bolton's Spicy Chicken & Fish, and 400 Degrees. At each place, the 'hot' chicken was delicious and impressively spicy, while the 'extra hot' was nearly unbearable. I remember watching Craig take a bite—his eyes became teary and his jaw began to quiver. . . I thought he was holding his breath, but the intake of heat from the chicken had hit his uvula and his tonsils and it knocked the wind out of him. It was about 15 seconds before he took another breath, and what for me seemed like a long time probably felt like an eternity to him. I always remember that when someone asks me 'Is it really hot?'"

Philadelphia chef Kevin Sbraga is perhaps best known for winning *Top Chef D.C.*, the seventh season of the long-running cooking competition program. While visiting his good buddy Arnold Myint, a fellow *Top Chef* alum and the proprietor of Nashville eateries PM, blvd, and Suzy Wong's House of Yum, Sbraga first ate Hot Chicken. He says he thought

Philadelphia's Spice. The Fat Ham's Hot Chicken wings are served on fresh, hand-sliced bread, with dill and pickles.

★MAINS★
NASHVILLE-HOT FRIED TURKEY
You'll be thankful for this spicy bird year round

Too few people eat turkey unless they're at a predictably awkward holiday meal. And too often those holiday birds are dried out and tasteless (which may explain why no one eats it otherwise). But here's an easy recipe that solves both problems. Deep frying until you hit the magic temperature keeps this bird juicy, and the spicy mix brushed on at the end ensures big flavor, whether it's Thanksgiving or not.

Deep frying turkey has gotten bad press over the years. Sure, cooking with an open flame and gallons of oil always leaves room for error. But as long as you cook outdoors and follow the manufacturer's instructions with your fryer, you'll be fine. In a nutshell—don't ever let open flame reach the oil itself, or do anything that might allow that to happen.

PREPARATION

Pour the oil into a deep propane turkey fryer, making sure it's at least 10 inches from the top of the pot. Follow the manufacturer's instuctions to reach and maintain the oil at 350°.

Prepare the turkey by removing the giblets and neck. Then rinse and pat dry. Mix the salt and pepper. Then coat the cavity and skin of the turkey and let rest at room temperature for 20-30 minutes.

Carefully lower turkey into the fryer until it is fully emerged. Some fryers are outfitted with fryer rods, others have large fry baskets. Whatever the case with your fryer, follow the manufacturer's instructions. Maintain oil temperature between 325° and 350° and cook until the thickest part of the thigh registers 165°. This is usually about 3 minutes per pound plus 5 additional minutes. A bird of this size will cook in roughly 45 minutes, but trust your thermometer; not the clock.

Remove the turkey from the oil and let stand for 30 minutes, reserving 1 cup of the hot oil.

While the turkey rests, mix the cayenne pepper, brown sugar, paprika, and garlic. Place the spice mixture in a saucepan over low heat and stir in 1 cup of oil from the fryer. Brush the spicy mixture all over the bird and serve immediately.

INGREDIENTS

- Peanut oil (about 3 gal.)
- 1 (12- to 14-lb.) whole fresh or frozen turkey, thawed
- 2 tablespoons salt
- 2 teaspoons ground black pepper
- ¼ cup ground cayenne pepper
- 1 tablespoon dark brown sugar
- 1 teaspoon paprika
- ½ teaspoon garlic powder

little of it at the time, and, moreover, wondered what all the fuss was about.

"It didn't have an immediate impact on me," Sbraga says. "It wasn't until a few days later, safe at home, that I started thinking about it. More importantly, I started *craving* it."

It wasn't long before Sbraga, who'd been musing on opening a second, more Southern-inspired eatery in Philadelphia, decided that his new restaurant, The Fat Ham, needed a showcase dish. Enter Hot Chicken.

"I wanted to bring something new to Philadelphia when I opened The Fat Ham," he says. "And the Hot Chicken was it. At the time, not many people were talking about it, so we were really the first in our area. Subsequently, we've become known for it now."

Sbraga says the success of other hot foods, and people's undying love of good fried chicken, above all, gave him the confidence to establish Hot Chicken as his latest restaurant's signature dish.

"Fried chicken will never go away," he says. "Essentially,

Hot Chicken is just a version of fried chicken. People love Buffalo wings, and once they take a bite of Hot Chicken, they love that too. It's not going anywhere. Our biggest challenge was presenting it in a way that looked classy."

INTERNATIONAL TWIST ON LOCAL FARE

Before she became known as Nashville's very own Raja of Ramen, Sarah Gavigan spent years as a music supervisor. While living in Los Angeles, she became obsessed with her then-hometown's thriving Japanese food culture—in particular, of the small-plates-with-drinks tapas-style *Izakaya* joints. So when she moved to Nashville, she began hosting popular pop-up events called Otaku South and serving her signature *izakaya* and fresh, regionally-sourced ramen at numerous local restaurants, including high-end spots like The Catbird Seat. This led to a four-days-a-week "permanent pop" pop-up restaurant at the dedicated pop-up spot in East Nashville, called, appropriately enough, POP.

She's since served Hot Chicken ramen at more than one pop-up (most notably with Hattie B's), and includes a Hot Chicken Bun (Hot Chicken on a steamed bao bun with dill pickle and kewpie slaw) on her regular menu.

"The first time I ever had Hot Chicken, it came from Prince's... as in 'Honey, me and the boys were at Prince's last night, and I saved you some.' I thought, come on...it's gimmicky. But spice never goes out of fashion in my world, and, that being said, what's wrong with being a food trend? As long as you are *good,* you stick around. I got curious and wanted to taste different takes on it."

Gavigan's Hot Chicken Bun is one of those takes—a sort of elevated and concentrated take on Nashville's famed foul.

 Some things never change. Whether highbrow or low, most versions of Hot Chicken thrive alongside familiar sides.

★ON THE SIDE★
MA'S SLAW
This vinegar-based side offers sweet relief

"Our grandmother has been making this sweet, vinegar-based slaw for over 70 years -- and it all started because of our grandfather's aversion to creamy slaw and all things mayonnaise. It's a simple recipe with straight-forward flavor, and a perfect compliment to the heat of Hot Chicken."

—Joe DeLoss, Hot Chicken Takeover, Columbus, OH.

PREPARATION

Dissolve sugar, salt, and pepper into apple cider vinegar. This should take several hours with frequent whisking. Mix dressing with half of your cabbage, allow to marinade for 6-12 hours. Add in remaining cabbage and serve. Add additional dressing to your liking.

INGREDIENTS

- 4 pounds shredded cabbage
- 1½ cups sugar
- 1 tablespoon kosher salt
- 1 tablespoon fine ground pepper
- 1½ cups apple cider vinegar

★MAINS★
HOT CHICKEN PIZZA
Two classic dishes come together as one

INGREDIENTS
FOR THE CRUST

- 3½ to 4 cups of all-purpose or bread flour
- 1¼ ounces instant dry yeast
- 1¼ cups warm water
- 1½ teaspoons sugar
- 1 tablespoon salt
- 2 tablespoons extra virgin olive oil, plus 2 teaspoons

TOPPINGS

- Prepared hot chicken rough cut into ½ inch cubes
- 8 ounces fresh mozzarella
- 4 ounces blue cheese
- Jalapeño peppers
- Chives, finely chopped
- Kosher dill pickles, finely chopped

Two Boots Pizza, a small chain with locations in New York City, Baltimore, Nashville, and Los Angeles, tailors its signature pizzas to its various locales. Nashville's offering is "The Kitty," after country music chanteuse Kitty Wells. "Kitty Wells revolutionized the role of women in country music," according to the restaurant, "and our tribute pie, The Kitty, is revolutionizing the role of hot chicken in Nashville." Two Boots tops their pizza with Hot Chicken from Hattie B's, and serves it with blue cheese and pickles (as seen at right). The pickles come on the side, in classic Hot Chicken fashion, and the heat is supplemented with jalapeños, which, of course, are not traditional. Then again, neither is Hot Chicken Pizza.

This recipe is inspired by Two Boots but I went ahead and threw the pickles on top. It's quick, it's easy, and, if you're looking for an extra kick with your pie, it's just the thing. Try this over a white pizza base, rather than marinara, to allow the chicken to be the star.

PREPARATION

Add the yeast to the water and let bloom while you combine flour, sugar, and salt in a stand mixer using a standard beater. (For crisper crust, opt for bread flour over all-purpose.) Switch to a dough hook and pour in the olive oil and the water/yeast mixture. Mix until the dough forms a ball. On a floured surface, knead dough into a smooth, firm ball. If it's too dry, add water 1 tablespoon at a time. If it sticks to your hands, add flour. Grease a bowl with oil, add dough, and cover. Let it rise a warm spot until it doubles in size—roughly 1 hour.

This makes two large pizzas or multiple smaller ones. Divide the dough, cover it, and let stand for 10 minutes. (To store a portion of dough, freeze it in an airtight container. When needed, it will thaw on your counter in about 2 hours.)

Preheat an iron skillet or flat grill pan over high heat. Roll the crust to desired thickness (for our purposes, thin works better). Precook crusts on the skillet until slightly browned. Then flip and repeat the process on the other side. The crusts are now ready for toppings.

Preheat the oven to 500°. Sauce the partially precooked crust with olive oil. Add the mozzarella, blue cheese crumbles, chopped chicken, pickles, and jalapeños. Cook until the cheese bubbles and begins to brown. As soon as it comes out of the oven, top with chives.

★ON THE SIDE★
LEGHORN CHICKEN'S BUTTERMILK BISCUITS
Because one Southern favorite deserves another

INGREDIENTS

MAKES 12 BISCUITS

- 4½ cups all purpose flour
- ⅛ cup plus 1½ teaspoons sugar
- ⅛ cup plus 1½ teaspoons baking powder
- 2 teaspoons Kosher salt
- ½ pound unsalted butter (cut into ½-inch cubes and frozen)
- 2 cups buttermilk
- ½ cup melted unsalted butter

By now, most folks see a good piece of fried chicken tucked between two halves of a buttery, flaky buttermilk biscuit as what it is: a meal equally at home in a picnic basket or white-tablecloth eatery, and suitable for breakfast, lunch, or dinner. Chicago's Leghorn Chicken offers another option in addition to the plain-Jane white bread usually served with Hot Chicken, and it's gaining followers by the week. Here's how to bake up a batch of your own.

PREPARATION

Preheat oven to 350°. Sift flour, sugar, baking powder and salt together. Cut in frozen butter until mixture resembles coarse cornmeal. Add buttermilk and gently work mixture until it becomes one homogenous mass. Roll out biscuits on a lightly floured surface to one-inch thickness. Cut out with a 3-inch round biscuit or cookie cutter. Place biscuits on parchment-lined sheet tray and bake for 10-15 minutes, or until golden brown. Remove biscuits from oven and immediately brush with the melted butter.

"I took the very popular and equally addictive version of Japanese fried chicken, *Karaage*, which is boneless, fry it, and toss it in our own twisty version of Japanese-meets-Kentucky-bourbon-meets-Hot-Chicken spices and serve it on a Chinese steamed white bread bun with Kewpie mayo. (It's) crunchy, spicy, and pillowy . . . it's as much a texture dish as it is a spice dish. That's why I love it."

HOT CHICKEN TAKES COLUMBUS

Joe DeLoss, who humbly describes himself as the "Head Fryer" at Columbus, Ohio's Hot Chicken Takeover, first tried Hot Chicken in November of 2013. DeLoss says he was as drawn to the sense of community Hot Chicken engendered as much as the dish itself.

"My wife and I took a 'babymoon' trip to Nashville in advance of our daughter's birth, and we instantly fell in love with the Hot Chicken experience. It was everything about it—the wait, the diverse crowd that gathered, and of course, the food. It was like nothing we'd ever eaten.

"We believe Hot Chicken is here to stay," he continues. "For many of our customers, their first experience with Hot Chicken means it's their last experience with conventional fried chicken. We spent the first few months of our trials just perfecting delicious *fried chicken*—everything from brines to buttermilk and more. With that behind us, then we went on to the secret sauce and found the perfect cayenne combo to serve as the base for our heat."

About that community DeLoss speaks of: Hot Chicken Takeover doesn't stop at serving a "diverse clientele"—a codeword oft-seen in newspaper articles and online hubs like Yelp.com meaning "you'll stand in line with people who don't always look like you or come from the same socio-economic class." DeLoss says he works with partners like Community Properties of Ohio and The Columbus Urban

COOP'S HOT CHICKEN PASTE
A jar of heat ready for export

Justin Williams and Jonathan Farmer invented Coop's Hot Chicken Paste after sensing a niche not being filled: what of folks who want to make their own Hot Chicken, but aren't handy in the kitchen? While they won't fry your chicken for you, and while they use ingredients like hydrogenated vegetable oil for greater shelf-life and stability, their concoction, with a few exceptions (see scorpion peppers), is relatively traditional, containing the usual cayenne, sugar, salt, and paprika. It's intended to be applied to your piping-hot chicken after frying, as is common in most Nashville-style joints. About a tablespoon per piece of chicken is the recommended amount; you simply warm the paste in the microwave to liquefy it, spread it on with a kitchen brush, and you're on your way.

Coop's is available at different foodsellers around Nashville, but those hungering for it outside of Middle Tennessee can cop a jar for $11 by going to coopshotchicken.com.

★MAINS★
HOT CHICKEN A LA LEGHORN
Chicago restraurant steps it up with a pickle brine

Chicago's Leghorn Chicken offers a little more variety than your typical Hot Chicken joint, but they don't let things get too out of hand. When you order, you specify your choice of pickle-brined chicken (a la Chick-fil-A) or Nashville Hot (either a boneless thigh or boneless breast), and then your choice of a house-made bun or buttermilk biscuit. Skip the optional toppings of cheese or tomato or slaw, however—their Hot Chicken is good enough to stand on its own.

PREPARATION

Brine chicken thighs in dill pickle juice in refrigerator for at least four hours. Prepare the seasoned flour by sifting all ingredients together. Mix the paste together and reserve. Slice a few of the pickles into thick sandwich slices.

Heat peanut oil to 350° in a Dutch oven. Dredge chicken thighs well in seasoned flour. Dust off any excess flour and drop into hot oil. The thighs will take about 7-10 minutes to cook to temperature (165°). Remove thighs from oil and drain on a rack. Immediately smear one tablespoon of the chili paste on each thigh. Slice biscuits in half lengthwise, and place one chicken thigh and two pickle slices on each biscuit. Top with the other biscuit half and serve immediately.

INGREDIENTS
SERVES 6

- 6 boneless organic chicken thighs (skin-on)
- Spicy dill pickles and brine (see recipe on page 114)
- Seasoned flour (recipe follows)
- Buttermilk biscuits (see recipe on page 104)
- Chili paste (recipe follows)
- 6-8 cups peanut oil (for frying)

SEASONED FLOUR

- 4 teaspoons white pepper
- 2 teaspoons cayenne
- 2 cups all-purpose flour
- 4 teaspoons paprika
- 2 tablespoons Kosher salt

CHILI PASTE

- ¼ cup schmaltz (melted)
- ½ cup Korean chili powder
- 3 teaspoons sugar
- 1 teaspoon salt
- ½ teaspoon garlic powder

CARLA HALL

The Nashville native shares her love for Hot Chicken

You may know Carla Hall from TV's *Top Chef* (she was a finalist in that show's fifth and eighth seasons), or from her role as co-host—with Michael Symon, Mario Batali and others—on ABC's *The Chew*. If you've lived in Nashville for a while, you might even know her personally—she was born and raised in Music City.

Thanks in part to a successful Kickstarter campaign, she's now about to be a restaurant owner/operator. Carla Hall's Southern Kitchen will feature as its signature dish none other than Nashville-style Hot Chicken, as well as a rotating array of sides including greens, mac and cheese, "picnic coleslaw," and Southern- or Southern-inspired desserts including red velvet whoopie pies and bread pudding. On weekends, you can even get your Hot Chicken served atop cornbread waffles.

Following, Hall takes a few minutes out of her busy schedule for a Hot Chicken heat check.

When did you first try Hot Chicken?

I can't quite remember, but I know I was in my teens. My first experience was at Prince's Hot Chicken. I was too young to appreciate that this was a "Nashville" thing. I'm always at mild. I'm not a hothead.

What made you decide on Hot Chicken as the focus of your new restaurant?

I'm from Nashville, and my restaurant concept, Carla Hall's Southern Kitchen, is a love letter to my hometown. When I decided to open a my first restaurant in New York City, it makes sense that I would share the same food that I grew up on and have written about in my cookbooks. I've made the menu simple, tight, and very focused, with Hot Chicken as the star—chicken and southern sides.

What made you feel that the time was right for a restaurant like this?

The media attention Hot Chicken has garnered has grown from the spotlight on Nashville's food scene in the last few years. As the love of the delicacy grows outside of Nashville city limits–throughout the U.S. and other parts of the world–eating spicy food has also become sport for some. The more people get used to eating full-flavored foods, not necessarily including spicy foods, the more flavor is needed to keep it interesting. That being said, I think that Hot Chicken has the same staying power as fried chicken. After all, at the end of the day, it's basically amped-up Southern fried chicken with various levels of heat. I think there are enough people who like spicy foods to support it.

Without giving away anything, how did you attempt to refine or bring your own touch to the dish?

Without changing Hot Chicken into something that it's not, or something that is too "cheffy," I'm planning to add an element of fruitiness to some of the hotter levels. I hope that the heat levels will be as flavorful as they are spicy.

League to refer potential employees who may have sketchy employment histories or criminal records, and works with these individuals through independent coaching and investment. Also, all Hot Chicken Takeover inventory that remains at the end of the day goes to local Faith Mission shelters.

After a series of successful pop-up events, Hot Chicken Takeover ran a Kickstarter campaign looking for $40,000 to run a "mobile unit"—a food truck, in the common parlance. Shocking even him, the campaign garnered over $63,000—some via large donations, but a lot of five-and-tenners in there as well—proving what he already guessed: people, of all varieties, are willing to vote with their pocketbooks for things they love, whether that means patronizing old favorites or supporting new ventures that fill a need.

"You just can't go back (once you've eaten Hot Chicken)," he says. "We've got way too many weekly customers to call it a 'stunt food'—between the community experience and the food, we think it's all pretty addictive."

HOT CHICKEN OVERSEAS

Hot Chicken's ever-expanding diaspora now includes locations serving Hot Chicken not just across the United States—Dallas, Chicago, New York City, Philadelphia, Portland, Boston, Austin—but the world. See Huckleberry Southern Kitchen and Bar in Davao, Phillipines, who serve "Nashville Hot Chicken Wings." Or former Husk Nashville chef Morgan McGlone's Belle's Hot Chicken, a dedicated Hot Chicken shack in Melbourne, Australia.

"We've received a tremendous amount of media attention from journalists, TV producers, authors, and foodies for our 'discovery'," says Ben Grossman of Peaches HotHouse in Brooklyn/Bed-Stuy. "When interviewed, we always give props to the originator, because, well, it's only right . . . and

★MAINS★
HOT CHICKEN STYLE PIG EARS
An upscale take on downhome ingredients

Thanks to the great work of sly Southerners like Hal Holden-Bache, the lowly pig ear is finally having its moment. Holden-Bache, executive chef and owner of Lockeland Table—a 2013 James Beard Awards Best New Restaurant nominee—likes to play on people's expectations. The restaurant is warm, comfortable, and unpretentious, much like its East Nashville neighborhood. One mainstay of the menu is the always popular Hot Pig Ears, which is exactly as it sounds: fried pig ears done up Nashville Hot Chicken style.

PREPARATION

Simmer the pig ears for seven to eight hours in salted water, and let them cool. Then julienne them very thinly, and fry them in batches. Toss them with the bacon fat and spices and serve over white bread with the gangster cabbage and thug pickles.

For the spice blend, mix together all dry spices. To make the paste, add 3½ cups Benton's bacon fat (or any other good bacon fat, melted) to spice blend until you achieve paste-like consistency. Add kosher salt to taste.

For the jalapeños, slice carrots and jalapeños ¼ inch thick. Boil remaining ingredients and pour over the jalapeños and carrots. Reserve in liquid, and pulse in food processor.

For the pickles, bring ingredients to a boil, and pour over cucumbers. Allow to cool.

SPICE BLEND
- 2 cups ground cayenne
- 1 cup ground paprika
- ¼ cup onion powder
- ¼ cup garlic powder
- ½ cup granulated sugar
- Kosher salt

GANGSTER CABBAGE
- 1 large head green cabbage
- 1 cup pimpin' jalapeños (see below)
- 2 tablespoons salt
- 2 tablespoons sugar
- 1½ cups apple cider vinegar

PIMPIN' JALAPENOS
- 3 lbs. jalapeños
- 2 lbs. carrots
- 1½ liters white wine
- 4 cups white vinegar
- 2 cups water
- 1 tablespoon sugar
- 1 tablespoon salt

THUG PICKLES
- 2 pounds English seedless cucumbers, sliced
- 1 white onion, peeled and julienned
- ¾ cup apple cider vinegar
- ¾ cup white vinegar
- 2 tablespoons salt
- 2 cups sugar
- 2 teaspoons celery seed
- 2 teaspoons mustard seed
- 1 teaspoon ground turmeric

Q&A: LINTON HOPKINS

Atlanta chef prefers a traditional cayenne heat

Over the last decade, James Beard Award winner Linton Hopkins—the chef and founder of Restaurant Eugene, Holeman & Finch, and the Peachtree Road Farmers Market, to name but a few—has become one of the icons of "new" local/seasonal Southern cooking. He's also not afraid to embrace newer arrivals to Southern culture.

"We're embracing every culture that comes through—it's not just about the new," Hopkins told *Condé Nast Traveler.* "Here, food removes barriers in a very ethnically diverse area. Southern cuisine is not just fried chicken and grits—that's part of our story, but it's not the end of our story."

An admitted fan of regional specialties, Hopkins jumped at the chance to talk Hot Chicken—certainly "not just" fried chicken—with us.

When did you first try Hot Chicken? What did you take away from the experience?
Five years ago, I was in Nashville doing an event, and someone brought in Prince's Hot Chicken for the chefs. I knew the legend of Prince's Hot Chicken from watching the Southern Foodways Alliance video, so I was forewarned about it being hot. I remember that first bite being crazy hot and yet deliciously addictive.

Do you believe Hot Chicken has staying power in the broader American food conversation?
I believe Hot Chicken is a dish that absolutely has staying power. Perhaps the broader national taste may stray from the "authentic," fiery-hot Nashville style to a milder version, but experiencing the variations of a dish is part of the fun of eating. It's a big world, and we should all play in it.

How much do you think this upward mobile export might have to do with Nashville's resurgence as a whole over the last five years or so?
Hot Chicken is just one component of Nashville's rich culinary scene. People are increasingly interested in the archeology of authentic food. Currently, there is a spotlight focused on Southern traditions like boudin and Hot Chicken. Nashville's rise in popularity may be tied to this focus, but I don't think it started the resurgence in Nashville, and I don't think the resurgence prompted people's love of Hot Chicken.

Are there any downsides to such a food becoming trendy?
I don't know if there's a downside to something people love becoming popular. There is a risk of menus lacking diversity if too many people jump aboard, but I think that

2277 PEACHTREE ROAD SUITE B

eventually works itself out. Recently pork bellies were everywhere, now it's Hot Chicken. A faithfully executed Hot Chicken will outlast the surge of a fad.

What inspired you when creating your own take on Hot Chicken?
The Hot Chicken on the menu at Holeman and Finch Public House is intended to pay homage to Prince's long-standing tradition, so I wanted it to be true to the original. My preferred preparation is one with a good, clean cayenne-based heat. I like the spice to be just hot enough that it starts to numb your mouth.

★ON THE SIDE★
LEGHORN'S SPICY DILL PICKLES
Homemade pickles dress up any dish

INGREDIENTS

- 5 pounds pickling cucumbers
- ¼ cup pickling spice
- 1 bunch fresh dill
- 3 ounces cider vinegar
- 3 ounces white distilled vinegar
- ¼ cup Korean chili powder
- ½ cup Kosher salt
- 10 cups water
- 10 cloves fresh garlic, peeled and left whole
- ⅛ cup dill seeds (lightly toasted)

No one can say for sure how the pickle became attached at the hip to Hot Chicken—most likely, it was a tossed-off throw-in that nobody thought much about until recently—but its place at the table in discussion of All Things Hot Chicken is assured. Tangy and salty and (most importantly) cooling on the tongue, pickles are a necessity at a true Hot Chicken joint, preferably dill, sliced thinly, and piled high. For a more artisanal take on the classic accompaniment, try this recipe from Chicago's Leghorn Chicken.

PREPARATION

Dissolve salt in water and vinegars. Layer cucumbers and remaining ingredients in a large crock. Cover with liquid and weight down so that all the cucumbers are completely submerged. Refrigerate for at least two weeks. (Pickles will hold for two months.)

relatively uncommon in this industry. One of the first commentsmade on Peaches HotHouse's Facebook page was from the original Prince's Hot Chicken Shack: 'Guess we should call you COUSIN. Glad we inspired your business and wish you all much success.' Though it's said that imitation is the sincerest form of flattery, I don't think anyone eating our chicken side by side would say they are the same thing—The HotHouse's chicken is an homage to Prince's original Hot Chicken, in the way that a Double Double Animal Style is a latter-day homage to Louis' Lunch."

"Every piece of chicken that I had at Prince's and Bolton's was crispy, juicy and delicious . . . and spicy." says Grossman. "As long as there are entire cultures and countries that embrace spice and heat, there will always be fresh takes on delivering that heat through delicious dishes. This is ours."

Indeed, the best of these new Hot Chicken outlets, will, either explicitly or in their preparation and care, echo the city of Nashville and its people. And hopefully, a little of their own city too. To follow a food's expansion across the country (and indeed the world) in real time is a rare opportunity we should savor, whether we trend towards the traditional or the avant-garde. One of the main benefits of our fast-moving, global food culture is not that the exotic is becoming more commonplace. It's that the commonplace can now be seen, and celebrated, as something exotic.

Originally concocted as a punishment, Hot Chicken is now a pleasure to be enjoyed by heatseekers everywhere. There is one constant, however, no matter how the dish is prepared, or where: Grab plenty of napkins, and, for heaven's sake, don't rub your eyes.

The future of Hot Chicken? Whether traditional takes on Hot Chicken are exported, as Joe DeLoss (below) did with Hot Chicken Takeover, or the flavors surface in unexpected dishes, as in Hal Holden-Bache's (right) Hot Pig Ears, Hot Chicken is here to stay.

THE JOINTS
Notable hot spots outside the Music City

BELLE'S HOT CHICKEN
(Melbourne, AUS)
Location: 150 Gertrude Street, Fitzroy
Vic, 3065, Australia
Phone: (03) 9077 0788
Web: belleshotchicken.com

CULLUM'S ATTAGIRL
(San Antonio, TX)
Location: 726 East Mistletoe, San
Antonio, Texas 78212
Phone: (210) 437-4263

THE FAT HAM
(Philadelphia, PA)
Location: 3131 Walnut Street
Philadelphia, PA 19104
Phone: (215) 735-1914
Web: sbragadining.com/fatham/

HOT CHICKEN TAKEOVER
(Columbus, OH)
Location: 59 Spruce Street, North
Market, Second Floor
Columbus, OH 43215
Phone: (614) 800-4538
Web: hotchickentakeover.com

HOWLIN' RAYS
(Los Angeles, CA)
Location: Los Angeles Food Truck,
location varies
Phone: (323) 823-7565
Web: howlinrays.com

JOELLA'S HOT CHICKEN
(Louisville, KY)
Location: 3400 Frankfort Avenue
Louisville, Kentucky 40207
Phone: (502) 895-2235
Web: joellashotchicken.com

LEGHORN CHICKEN
(Chicago, IL)
Location: 959 North Western Avenue
Chicago, Illinois 60622
Phone: (773) 394-4444
Web: leghornchicken.com

PEACHES HOTHOUSE
(Brooklyn, NY)
Location: 415 Tompkins Avenue,
Brooklyn, NY 11216
Phone: (718) 483-9111
Web: bcrestaurantgroup.com/hothouse

RAPSCALLION
(Dallas, TX)
Location: 2023 Greenville Avenue
#103 Dallas, Texas 75001
Phone: (469) 291-5660
Web: dallasrapscallion.com

THE ROOST CAROLINA KITCHEN
(Chicago, IL)
Location: 1467 W Irving Park Road,
Chicago, IL 60613
Phone: (312) 261-5564
Web: theroostcarolinakitchen.com

STATE PARK
(Cambridge, MA)
Location: Building 300, 1 Kendall
Square Cambridge, MA 02139
Phone: (617) 848-4355
Web: statepark.is

SUPER CHIX
(Arlington, TX)
Location: 612 W Park Row Dr #620,
Arlington, Texas 76010
Phone: (817) 795-1828
Web: superchix.com

THUNDERBIRD
(Indianapolis, IN)
Location: 1127 Shelby Street,
Indianapolis, IN 46203
Phone: (317) 974-9580
Web: thunderbirdindy.com

YARD HOUSE
(Addison, TX)
Location: 5100 Belt Line Rd Addison,
TX 75001
Phone: (972) 716-4004
Web: yardhouse.com

ZINGERMAN'S ROADHOUSE
(Ann Arbor, MI)
Location: 2501 Jackson Ave, Ann
Arbor, MI 48103
Phone: (734) 663-3663
Web: zingermansroadhouse.com

CHAPTER FOUR
THE COOL DOWN ❄

DESSERTS THAT OFFER SWEET RELIEF

It's no exaggeration to say that Lisa Donovan is one of the best pastry chefs in America. Her career includes stops at three of Nashville's—hell, the country's—best restaurants: City House, Margot, and Husk Nashville. She's the founder and chief strategist behind the wildly successful pop-up restaurant series Buttermilk Road Sunday Supper.

If that's not enough, Donovan is also a wonderfully skilled writer, bringing a chef-like focus on nuance, sincerity, humor, and genuine human connection to her pieces, whether for her blog or magazines like *Saveur* and *Food & Wine*.

Following, in Donovan's own words, are two recipes she formulated specifically for this book, along with recipe notes for each. ➡

★DESSERTS★
FROM-SCRATCH BANANA PUDDING
Pick pudding for a perfect finish

Desserts aren't a highlight of most Hot Chicken shacks. You'll find a slice of pie here and there and maybe even a piece of locally-made layer cake. But, I think it's fair to say that, unlike the traditional southern meat and threes where desserts are chosen alongside the meats and sides themselves, Hot Chicken doesn't care what you do after you've eaten it. Hot Chicken assumes you'll be done eating for a while. Hot Chicken is in the conquering business. So when Tim asked me to think about desserts in the Hot Chicken world, I came to one conclusion: you want a smooth operator, a Sade-style songstress that can ease you back down from the "romp on the hood of your car" craziness that is Hot Chicken.

Pudding. Pudding is that sweet seductress. I think there is a distinct reason why Southerners love a pudding. In fact, there are many reasons, but the main one, I believe, has everything to do with it's effect of being light and cool after a heavy meal of fried and cured meats, rolls, and long-cooked vegetables. Having something as borderline ethereal as a pudding with meringue on top can seemingly wind down a meal that was simultaneously gratifying as hell and a bit burdensome on the gut. Sometimes, especially if you've chosen "hot," a small spoonful of the simplest pudding is all you need to move along and keep you going until the next time you are foolhardy enough to wander back down Ewing Drive, look Ms. Andre in the face, and say "hot, please" once again.

—Lisa Donovan

- 1 large whole egg
- 4 egg yolks (reserving whites for meringue)
- ¾ cup sugar
- ¼ cup all-purpose flour
- 1 teaspoon salt
- 2 cups whole milk
- 1 cup heavy cream
- Scraping of one vanilla bean or two teaspoons vanilla paste
- 40 vanilla wafers (recipe below)
- 4 medium-sized ripened bananas, sliced 1/8"

MERINGUE
- 4 egg whites (reserved from above)
- Pinch of salt
- ¼ teaspoon cream of tartar
- ½ cup sugar

In a saucepan, warm the whole milk and vanilla, careful not to scald. In a separate bowl, make your slurry by whisking together the sugar, flour and salt. Add the whole egg and yolks and whisk. Whisk in the cream. Once the milk is hot, slowly temper into the slurry. Return all ingredients to the saucepan and, stirring constantly, cook on medium until thickened. Strain through a chinois.

Preheat oven to 450°. Layer your pudding into a 2 quart oven-proof casserole dish starting with a thin layer of pudding. Top thin layer of pudding with vanilla wafers, covering the bottom. Top wafers with banana. Then, top with a third of your pudding. Repeat wafer and banana layer and complete building layers in thirds ending with pudding.

To make meringue: whisk reserved egg white, salt and tartar until they become medium-firm peaked. Turn whisk to medium low and add sugar slowly. Turn whisk up to high and beat until a glossy sheen comes over your meringue. Spread over final layer of casserole. Bake for 5-7 minutes until meringue is browned.

VANILLA WAFERS

- 7 ounces all purpose flour
- ¾ teaspoon baking powder
- ¼ teaspoon baking soda
- ¾ teaspoon salt
- 4 ounces unsalted butter
- 3 ounces pure cane sugar
- 2 vanilla beans
- 1 egg
- 4 teaspoons vanilla extract
- 1 tablespoon whole-fat buttermilk

Scrape vanilla beans into pure cane sugar and rub together to break up vanilla bean seeds into sugar. In a separate bowl, combine all dry ingredients. Cream butter and vanilla sugar together in mixer with paddle until slightly fluffy. Add egg and continue to cream until full incorporated. Add milk and vanilla extract and continue creaming. Add dry to combine. Chill for at least 10 minutes. Scoop 1 tablespoon rounds onto a sheet pan covered with a Silpat (or parchment sprayed with baking spray) and, with a damp palm, slightly press down on dough to create a bit of a flat disc shape. Sprinkle with plain sugar or make more vanilla sugar to use. Bake at 350° for 8-10 minutes.

★DESSERTS★
SPICED CRUZE'S BUTTERMILK SHAKE
Nothing beats sweet dairy to cool things down

Let's not fool ourselves. There is little to do about the hallucinatory and painfully thrilling ride that is Hot Chicken while you're strapped in—pickle slices only do so much. But if I've learned anything over the course of the last decade as a true-blue Nashville Hot Chicken consumer, it's that I prefer my Hot Chicken "picnic" style (that's refrigerator cold or at least room temperature, for you non-Southerners), and I prefer it with a milkshake of some kind.

I developed this recipe with two things in mind: the first time I tasted Cruze's buttermilk eight years ago in the kitchen when I was the pastry chef at City House, and how much I appreciate the cooling effects of a horchata when I'm indulging in spicy Mexican food. I kind of wanted an uber-effect of the two combined in an ice cream milk shake.

This is an easy recipe to tweak and play around with. For example, I happen to be lucky enough to live near a Mexican market that sells horchata that is a bit fuller fat than most horchatas—though, they won't tell me why it's so rich and delicious and I've decided to quit asking—and it makes for a great liquid to add to the final step of turning the ice cream into a shake versus the half and half. Also, feel free to play around with the spices—taste as you go and adjust according to your preference.

—Lisa Donovan

FOR THE ICE CREAM

- 3 cups heavy cream
- 2 cups sugar
- 10 egg yolks
- 1 vanilla bean, scraped (or 2 teaspoons vanilla paste)
- 2 cups Cruze's buttermilk or other full fat buttermilk
- Small pinch salt

Warm cream, sugar and vanilla bean (scrapings and bean) in saucepan until sugar dissolves and is completely warmed. In a separate bowl, whisk egg yolks together. When cream and sugar are hot, slowly temper into the yolks by whisking half of cream slowly into the bowl. Combine the tempered yolks and cream into the pan with remaining cream sugar mixture. Stir constantly on medium low until the mixture coats the back of a spoon evenly. Strain through a chinois and place a piece of plastic wrap directly on top of the mixture. Chill completely and then freeze according to manufacturer label of your ice cream maker.

FOR THE SHAKE

In a blender, combine one teaspoon cinnamon, 4-5 ounces of half and half, three grates of fresh nutmeg and two 4 ounce scoops of ice cream. Blend until combined, adding more liquid to achieve the consistency you like. Serve with whipped cream and a few shakes of cinnamon on top.

COPYRIGHT & PHOTO CREDITS

Publisher: Paul McGahren
Editor: Matthew Teague
Interior Design: Benjamin Rumble
Cover Design: Lindsay Hess
Photographer: Danielle Atkins, except where noted

Spring House Press
3613 Brush Hill Court
Nashville, TN 37216

ISBN: 978-1-940611-19-8
Library of Congress Control Number: 2015951464
Printed in the United States of America
Third Printing

Note:
The following list contains names used in The Hot Chicken Cookbook
that may be registered with the United States Copyright Office:
A.1. Steak Sauce, Aldi, Blackbird, Blue Plate, Chick-fil-A, Condé Nast Traveler, Coop's, Cleveland Browns, Cruze, Duke's, Facebook, The Food Network, *Food Republic*, Gawker, Grand Ole Opry, Grub Street, Hair World, Heinz, Kewpie, Hellman's, Houston Texans, Lincoln, Lowry's, Morrison's, National Basketball Association, *The New York Times*, The Oprah Network, PBS, Quizno's, Silpat, Southern Foodways Alliance, Sweetie Pies, Tabasco, Tennessee Titans, *The Wall Street Journal*

To learn more about Spring House Press books, or to find a retailer near you, email info@springhousepress.com or visit us at: www.springhousepress.com.

ACKNOWLEDGEMENTS

My sincere thanks to everyone who took the time to speak with me for this book—if your graciousness is any indication, the future of Hot Chicken is indeed a bright one. Thanks to my amazing family—father Jerry, mother Alice and brother Patrick—for the love and support and for making this guy recognize the special majesty of a great book, and for all those many rides to the library. Thanks to Andre Prince Jeffries, Simone Jeffries, Isaac Beard, Aqui Powell, Nick Bishop Jr., Hal Holden-Bache, and all the other restaurateurs here in Nashville keeping the "Nashville Hot" faith. Thanks to Matthew Teague and Paul McGahren at Spring House Press for believing in this book and, moreover, this writer. Thanks to Danielle Atkins and Benjamin Rumble for making this book come to life with your obvious talents—I owe y'all one. Thanks to Mike House and his family, Philip Blumenthal, and all at Wildacres Retreat for the residency—this book was birthed in your beautiful artist's sanctuary. Thanks to Elissa Schappell for helping me dig deeper. Thanks to John T. Edge for his encouragement and example over the years—I'm in your debt, and hope I'm helping to repay it. Thanks to Ronni Lundy for the inspiration and steerage, whether in person or on the page. Thanks to Andrew Zimmern for going above and beyond the call of duty—your next order of Hot Chicken is on me, good sir. Thanks to Carla Hall for her kind words and valuable time—you do Nashville proud. My gratitude to Janey Klebe, Jen van Kaam, and Kirsten Bischoff—y'all deserve a long round of applause. Thanks to the amazing Lisa Donovan for the sweet(s), last-second assist. Thanks to all those fine-fettled friends who've been there for me over lo these many years—folks including Stephanie Koehler, Tim Long, Shawn Lynch, Katherine Everhart, John Schacht, Catie Cameron, Kyle Frohock, Evan Brown, CT Stephenson, Faith Wally, Aereal Davis, Alan Edwards, Heidi McGlothlin, Blake Boldt, Bill W., Jennifer Larson, Kathleen Cotter, and Jake Girardin, to name but a very few—my space is limited, but y'all know who you are, and I'm certainly aware. Thanks to the LeCoguic/Green families for accepting me as one of your own. Thanks to Bill Purcell, who, were there ever such a thing, would be a first-ballot inductee to the Hot Chicken Hall of Fame. Thanks to Kim Prince and the Heritage Foundation of Franklin and Williamson County for the use of the Thornton Prince picture. Thanks to my fellow food scribes Kathleen Purvis, Carrington Fox, Jennifer Justus, Nicki Pendleton Wood, Chris Chamberlain and Dana Kopp Franklin for all of their help, guidance and table-sharing. Thanks to my many exemplary editors over the years, a (patient) list that includes John Grooms—who saw something in me when I had yet to—Ann Wicker, Matt Brunson, Mark Kemp, Ron Charles, Fred Mills, Steven Shaw (R.I.P.), Kent Kimes and Sara Roahen, as well as Chuck Allen, Erin Murray and Jim Ridley here in Nashville. Special thanks to Robin Murphree for always being there for me when it counted, and moreover for helping keep me here in beautiful Nashville, Tennessee—I couldn't have done it without you, my dear. Furry and purr-y thanks to B. Bisters. Extra special thanks to Matthew Butcher—I love you, brother. Last but not least, thank you to the incomparable Coralie LeCoguic for being my everything, all the time. This book is for you, my love.

INDEX

ABOUT THE AUTHOR

Timothy Charles Davis has written for a host of outlets, including *Saveur*, the *Christian Science Monitor*, *Gastronomica*, *Mother Jones*, Salon.com, and *The Oxford American*. He is a former staff writer and food columnist at *Creative Loafing* in Charlotte, NC and *Weekly Surge* in Myrtle Beach, SC. He contributed as an associate editor for *Gravy*, the official magazine of the Southern Foodways Alliance, and was also a co-writer of *The Southern Foodways Alliance Community Cookbook*. He lives in Nashville, TN, where he's written for outlets including *Nashville Scene*, *Nashville Lifestyles*, and *The East Nashvillian*, and worked in more restaurant kitchens than he'd care to mention. He's a "hot, extra bread, extra pickles" kind of guy, sometimes dropping down to a "medium" for a few weeks in the interest of self-preservation.